best ever

 chocolate

p

This is a Parragon Book
First published in 2003

Parragon
Queen Street House
4 Queen Street
Bath BA1 1HE
United Kingdom

Created and produced by
The Bridgewater Book Company Ltd,
Lewes, East Sussex

Photographer David Jordan
Home economist Judy Williams
Thanks are due to Moulinex and Tower Pans for supplying equipment

ISBN: 1–40540–521–X

Printed in China

NOTE

This book uses metric and imperial measurements. Follow the same units
of measurement throughout; do not mix metric and imperial. All spoon
measurements are level: teaspoons are assumed to be 5 ml and tablespoons are
assumed to be 15 ml. Unless otherwise stated, milk is assumed to be full fat and
eggs and individual fruits such as bananas are medium.

The times given for each recipe are an approximate guide only
because the preparation times may differ according to the techniques used
by different people, and the cooking times may vary as a result of the type of
oven used. Ovens should be preheated to the specified temperature. If using a
fan-assisted oven, check the manufacturer's instructions for adjusting the time
and temperature. The preparation times include cooling, chilling and freezing
times, where appropriate. Optional ingredients, variations or serving
suggestions have not been included in the calculations.

Recipes using raw or very lightly cooked eggs should be avoided
by infants, the elderly, pregnant women, convalescents and anyone
suffering from an illness.

contents

introduction

Chocolate seems to have a special power unlike that of any other food. Chemists are still not certain what is in the composition of chocolate that makes it quite so irresistible to so many people. To say that consuming chocolate can become an addiction is not an exaggeration, since chocolate contains a natural amphetamine that stimulates the nervous system to produce a feeling of well-being, and it also contains theobromine and caffeine, which are both stimulants. Its smooth texture and the fact that it melts at blood temperature make it deliciously seductive.

Few people can resist a chocolate dessert or cake, but tend to think that the art of chocolate cooking is strictly for the experts. This book aims to dispel that myth with recipes that, although they look impressive, do not require any complicated techniques or skills other than a love of good food and a desire to delight family and friends. This collection offers recipes suitable for every occasion, together with ideas for making simple confectionery and drinks. These opening pages also present a guide to the various types of chocolate and how to choose and store it, as well as simple instructions for melting chocolate and making easy yet effective chocolate decorations.

And there is no need to feel too guilty about eating chocolate, because it is nutritious! It yields up to 600 calories of energy per 100 g/3½ oz, mostly in the form of fat, sugar, protein and iron. This is why it is included in the survival kits of soldiers and mountaineers.

the history of chocolate

The cacao or cocoa tree has been cultivated since the 7th century and is native to Central and South America. Its botanical name is *Theobroma cacao*, which means 'food of the gods'.

The chocolate we know today bears little resemblance to xocoatl, the infusion drunk by the Aztecs, Mayans and Incas. This was extremely bitter and often flavoured with spices, including chilli. A froth, which was the most desirable part of the drink, was achieved by pouring it from a height. Cacao beans were valued highly and used as currency. Because of its value, chocolate had great ceremonial importance and was served at banquets, offered to the gods and used to anoint newborn babies.

The first Europeans to see the cacao bean were those on Columbus's fourth voyage to the New World in 1502, when he captured a Mayan trading canoe laden with cacao beans and other treasures. However, although he knew of their value as currency, he failed to discover that a drink could be made from them. It was not until 20 years later, when the Spaniards under Cortés invaded Mexico, that the true worth of these black 'almonds' was revealed. At first the conquistadores were disgusted by the dark, bitter drink, but they soon learned to appreciate it, especially when they heard rumours of its aphrodisiac qualities. Cortés took some beans with him when he returned home, planting some in Africa on the way. Sugar and milder spices such as vanilla and cinnamon were added and the Spanish quickly became addicted to it. Preachers railed against it from the pulpit, as ladies were unable to resist sipping it throughout the sermon.

The Spanish king and his court guarded the secret of the delights of chocolate until 1606, when Antonio Carlutti took it to Italy. From then on, the pleasures of drinking chocolate spread quickly across Europe, and Italian cooks began to experiment with adding chocolate as a flavouring in savoury and sweet dishes, including sorbets and ice cream.

At the beginning of the 17th century, this exciting new drink was an expensive luxury appreciated only by the aristocrats of European courts, but soon chocolate houses were springing up all over Europe and they became established as meeting places for fashionable intellectuals. When chocolate houses appeared in London, as predecessors to gentlemen's clubs, they were briefly banned by Charles II as hotbeds of radical politics. The Cocoa Tree Chocolate House, which later became the Garrick Club, was an early headquarters of the Jacobite party, and White's Chocolate House was a headquarters for the Whigs, and later the Tories. These chocolate houses were frequented by Samuel Pepys and many poets, playwrights and would-be politicians.

The chocolate drink enjoyed at this time was made from a crumbly coarse paste with a high fat content. Two centuries later, a Dutchman called C. J. van Houten developed a screw press that removed the fat or cocoa butter from the beans, leaving a powdery residue, which became known as cocoa. This dispersed easily in water and was considered more digestible than full-fat chocolate. A use was soon found for the excess cocoa butter when the English firm, Fry & Sons, added sugar and chocolate liquor to the cocoa butter to produce the first eating chocolate. Prices remained high due to the import duty levied on cacao beans, but this was reduced in 1853 and imports of cheap sugar also helped lower the price. Nonetheless, chocolate remained a luxury.

In the early days, all eating chocolate was plain with a rough, grainy texture. The first milk chocolate was made in Switzerland, using dried milk, which was a new product manufactured by Henri Nestlé. Milk and chocolate liquor were mixed and dried, then cocoa butter added, in a process very similar to the modern 'milk crumb' process. The Swiss dominated the market for milk chocolate until the early 20th century and continued to improve their recipe until it became the smooth, melting chocolate we know today.

Chocolate became available to a wider audience when it was included in rations for the troops during World War I. After the war, the price of chocolate continued to fall as the price of goods came down and technological advances reduced manufacturing costs. By the beginning of World War II, chocolate confectionery was outselling sugar confectionery – and has continued to do so.

producing chocolate

The cacao tree, *Theobroma cacao*, is cultivated in the tropical zone within 20° of the equator. It requires year-round moisture and a temperature that never falls below 18°C/64°F. West Africa produces 60 per cent of the world's supply of cocoa, while Brazil is the largest producer in South America. The trees, which are cultivated under banana or rubber trees to provide shade, start producing pods when they are three to five years old. Although the flowers bloom throughout the year, only about 30 flowers per tree produce red or yellow spindle-shaped pods or fruits, which grow directly out from the trunk. Each pod contains 30–40 white or purple seeds – the cacao beans.

After harvesting, the pods are split open and the contents are scraped out. The seeds and surrounding pulp are piled up on banana or plantain leaves and covered with a layer of damp leaves. They are then left in the sun to ferment for five to six days. As they ferment, the pulp turns to liquid and drains away, and the beans turn a dark brown. This fermentation is essential to allow a good flavour to develop. After fermentation, the beans are left to dry in the sun, then they are exported to the manufacturing country to be turned into the chocolate bars we know and love.

After cleaning, the first stage in processing is roasting, which further develops the cocoa flavour. Then the kernels or 'nibs' are extracted from the beans and ground by metal mills with sophisticated temperature controls. The grinding process extracts the cocoa butter, leaving a thick paste – the chocolate liquor. This hardens on cooling to form unsweetened cooking chocolate. Further pressing extracts even more cocoa butter and the solid cake that remains is ground into cocoa powder. To make plain chocolate for eating, extra cocoa butter and sugar are added to the chocolate liquor. Dried milk is added to make milk chocolate.

The next process is known as 'conching'. The semi-liquid mixture is poured into machines that constantly knead the mass at a temperature of 55–85°C/131–185°F. This evaporates moisture, improves the texture and develops the flavour and can take from several hours to a week, depending on the quality required. Towards the end of conching, the desired flavours are added. Vanilla is the most common in European and North American chocolate, but other flavours such as mint, coffee and orange are also popular.

Before chocolate is moulded into bars or used for coating, it is tempered by cooling very carefully to 26°C/79°F. This further improves the texture, gloss and keeping qualities of chocolate.

types of chocolate

Bitter chocolate is unsweetened chocolate for cooking. It is not widely available but is excellent in baking.

Chocolate couverture is chocolate with a very high cocoa butter content and is generally available only to professional confectioners. It flows very smoothly, making it ideal for coating purposes. It is available in plain and milk forms, but is usually expensive.

Plain chocolate is the most useful type of chocolate for cooking, as it gives a good strong chocolate flavour. Good-quality chocolate is now widely available in supermarkets. To assess a chocolate's quality, read the label and look for a high cocoa-solid content – the best chocolate contains 50 per cent or more. However, chocolate with cocoa solids above 65 per cent can be an acquired taste, as it tends to be extremely intense and bitter. Buy the best-quality chocolate you can afford – it will show in the texture, flavour and appearance of the finished dish. Milk chocolate is not a satisfactory substitute in most recipes, as it is very sweet and does not give such a strong flavour. It is effective piped on to plain chocolate for decoration and may be used for moulding Easter eggs for children. Look for a cocoa solid content of 40 per cent in milk chocolate.

White chocolate is not strictly chocolate at all, as it contains cocoa butter, milk and sugar but no chocolate liquor. It is not normally used in cooking because of its lack of flavour, but its creamy consistency makes it suitable for use in cold desserts, and it makes a good contrast when combined with plain chocolate.

Ready-made chocolate-flavoured cake covering is not recommended for the recipes in this book. It contains a minimum of 2.5 per cent cocoa solids, and vegetable oil instead of added cocoa butter. It is considerably cheaper than real chocolate, but its flavour and texture are inferior. However, chocolate-flavoured cake covering can be easier to use than real chocolate, as it is easier to melt. It is more fluid than melted chocolate, and sets quickly when used for coating.

Cocoa powder is an inexpensive and convenient way of achieving a strong chocolate flavour in baking, but it is not suitable for use in uncooked dishes, as it has a powdery texture. A good substitute for bitter chocolate is to mix together 3 tablespoons of cocoa powder and 1 tablespoon of butter. Add 1 tablespoon of sugar to make a substitute for plain chocolate.

Drinking chocolate is a mixture of cocoa and sugar, and is generally too sweet for use in cooking unless the sugar in the recipe is reduced accordingly.

Carob is not chocolate at all, but is a member of the legume family. However, processed carob and chocolate have similarities, so it deserves a mention in this book. Carob is grown all over the Mediterranean and in the United States. The pods, which resemble broad beans, develop into dark brown leathery pods with a glossy surface. The seeds are processed and used as a gelling agent, while the pods are roasted, milled and sieved to produce carob powder, which can be used in cooking. Powdered carob is made into bars by mixing with raw cane sugar, vegetable fats, skimmed milk powder, lecithin and flavouring. Carob is rich in vitamins and minerals, contains no refined sugar, theobromine, caffeine or oxalic acid and contains fewer calories than chocolate. It can be substituted for chocolate in many recipes, although it will not have the shiny finish of chocolate when melted, and for chocolate-lovers it is no substitute for the real thing!

choosing and storing chocolate

When unwrapped, the surface of chocolate should be glossy and smooth. Plain chocolate should be deep mahogany, never black. When you break a bar of chocolate, it should give a crisp snap and there should be a tree-bark texture in the break. When you allow a piece of chocolate to melt on your tongue, it should have a clean taste and the aroma might conjure up caramel, wood, fruit, flowers or spice. It should be creamy, not oily, and it should melt quickly, which is an indication of a high level of cocoa butter.

When kept in the right conditions, plain and milk chocolate will have a shelf life of about one year, but white chocolate tends to deteriorate after about eight months. It should be well wrapped and stored in a cool, dry place, ideally at 16–18°C/61–64°F. 'Bloom' is the greyish-white coating that appears on the surface of chocolate which has not been stored correctly. Although this looks unattractive, it does not affect the flavour and it is not an indication that the chocolate has 'gone off'. Chocolate stored at below 13°C/55°F will usually develop a bloom and will 'sweat' when returned to room temperature. Chocolate stored at too high a temperature will also develop a bloom.

'Fat bloom' is caused by heating and cooling chocolate. It is quite greasy and rubs off the surface of the chocolate very easily. 'Sugar bloom' shows as a white crust of sugar crystals on chocolate that has been stored in a refrigerator.

chocolate in cooking

In European and North American cuisine, chocolate is widely used as a flavouring for puddings, desserts, cakes, biscuits and ice cream, and it is often combined with nuts, fruit, orange, mint, coffee and spirits. In the form of cocoa, it provides a concentrated flavour and is used in baking and icings. Melted block chocolate is used for richer cakes and to flavour creams, mousses, soufflés, sauces and ice creams.

Chocolate is more usually thought of as an ingredient solely for use in sweet dishes, but it can be used to flavour savoury dishes, such as sauce for game and the famous Mexican mole sauces. It adds depth of flavour and darkness to a sauce. It is thought that in Europe it was the Italians who first started using chocolate in savoury dishes, such as meat pasties, and it is still used in Italy in the sweet and sour salsa agrodolce, which is served with wild boar and hare. The Spanish took up the idea and there are still Catalan dishes that are seasoned with chocolate. It is used more widely in Latin American dishes, which is a reflection of the Spanish influence.

how to melt chocolate

Chocolate scorches very easily if it is heated above 44°C/111°F, and will 'seize' into hard, grainy lumps. This will also happen if any liquid or steam comes into contact with the chocolate while it is melting. If the chocolate does seize, there is usually nothing that can be done to make it usable again, but it is worth adding a little oil, which sometimes helps to restore it. Extra care should be taken when melting white chocolate, as it is extremely sensitive to heat.

Chocolate can be safely melted with a small amount of liquid, such as milk, cream, water or alcohol, if they are placed in the bowl together. It will melt more quickly and evenly if the chocolate is first broken into small pieces. Avoid stirring the chocolate until it has melted and then stir it very gently with a wooden spoon until smooth.

Chocolate can be added to a large quantity of hot liquid and left to melt without stirring. Stir very gently, when completely melted, to make a smooth mixture.

There are several different ways of melting chocolate. The methods described below are the most successful.

Over hot water: break the chocolate into small pieces, then place in a small heatproof bowl and set over a saucepan of gently simmering water, making sure that the base of the bowl does not come into contact with the water. Remove the saucepan from the heat and leave until the chocolate has melted.

In the oven: place the chocolate in a small, shallow ovenproof dish and heat in a preheated oven, 110°C/225°F/Gas Mark ¼, until the chocolate has melted.

In a microwave oven: place the chocolate in a microwaveproof bowl and heat for 1–2 minutes in a microwave oven on full power, stirring gently occasionally, until the chocolate has melted. The exact time depends on the quantity of chocolate,

the size of the bowl and the power of the oven. When melting white chocolate in the microwave, set the oven on 50 per cent power and use it in 1 minute bursts, stirring the chocolate at each interval.

In a polythene bag: this is a clean and convenient way of melting a small amount of chocolate, particularly if it is to be used for piping a decoration (see pages 11–12). Place the chocolate in a small polythene food bag, seal and place the bag in a saucepan of hot water. When the chocolate has melted, cut a corner off the bag and pipe as required.

tips on using melted chocolate

• Leave melted chocolate to cool slightly before adding to other ingredients.
• Adding a small quantity of butter or oil to the chocolate will make it much smoother and more fluid for coating and dipping.
• Add chocolate to other liquid ingredients rather than pouring the other liquid into the chocolate.
• When using melted chocolate in cake mixtures, add it to the creamed mixture before incorporating the eggs and flour.
• In mousse and soufflé mixtures, blend the melted chocolate with the egg yolks and flavouring before adding the cream and egg whites.

making decorations

When you have gone to all the trouble of making a wonderful chocolate cake, pudding or dessert, an attractive decoration will add the finishing touch and make it look all the more professional. Some chocolate decorations can be rather tricky to make at first and will require a little practice before you achieve exactly the desired effect. Others are very easy and straightforward. If you are not very confident, experiment first with chocolate cake covering, as it is easier

to work with than good-quality chocolate. Even if you do have a disaster, you can always re-melt the chocolate and make another attempt. Leave decorations in a cool place to set, but do not put them in the refrigerator or they will develop an unattractive 'bloom'.

Some of the easiest decorations to make are described below, including chocolate curls, grated chocolate and chocolate leaves. Half-coating fruit, such as strawberries, is also easy and effective. These not only look good on top of cakes, but taste delicious.

Grated chocolate: This is one of the easiest and most effective chocolate decorations to make at home. Depending on the coarseness of the grater used, a variety of effects, from a fine chocolate powder to coarse curls, can be achieved. Grated chocolate can be sprinkled over a dessert or used to cover the top and sides of a cake that has been coated in cream or buttercream. Alternate lines of grated white and plain chocolate can be very attractive as a decoration. Roll home-made truffles in finely grated plain, milk or white chocolate.

Chocolate curls: Use a thick bar of chocolate that has been softened very slightly. It must not be too cold or too warm, and it is only through trial and error that you will achieve the right condition. Run a vegetable peeler down the side of the chocolate bar and allow the curls to fall on to a plate. Lift them carefully on to the cake or dessert that is to be decorated.

Chocolate caraque: Spread a thin layer of melted chocolate on to a flat surface, preferably marble, and just when it appears to have set, but is in fact still soft, hold a knife or scraper at a 45° angle to the surface and push it along to form long scrolls. As the curls form, lift them carefully with the point of a knife. Caraque may be kept in a box in the refrigerator for a short while, if necessary, until required.

Chocolate leaves: Chocolate leaves are easy to make, and any fresh leaves may be used as long as they are not poisonous. Choose leaves that have prominent veins and are an attractive shape. Rose leaves are ideal. Wash and dry the leaves thoroughly, then brush the underside with melted chocolate. Place the chocolate-coated leaves on a sheet of non-stick baking paper until completely set, then gently lift the tip of the leaf and peel it away from the chocolate.

Chocolate shapes: For squares, diamonds and triangles, spread a thin layer of melted chocolate on to a sheet of non-stick baking paper and leave until just set. Using a ruler and a sharp knife, trim the chocolate into a square, then carefully cut into smaller squares, diamonds or triangles. Leave in a cool place until completely set before carefully removing from the paper. For other shapes, use a metal biscuit or pastry cutter. Aspic cutters are ideal for tiny decorations. These thin chocolate shapes go stale quickly, so they should not be kept for long before use. Because they are very fragile, it is advisable to keep them in an airtight box in the refrigerator. As long as they are left at room temperature to set, and are not stored for long, they are unlikely to develop a bloom.

Chocolate cups: Coat the inside of double-thickness paper cake cases or petit four cases with cooled melted chocolate. Spread the chocolate evenly inside the cases with a brush or spoon. Leave to set, then add another layer if desired. It is better to brush on two thin layers rather than one thick layer. Leave the cups in a cool place until set hard, then carefully peel away the paper. Chocolate cups make edible containers for fruit and cream, mousse mixtures or ice cream, and smaller ones can be filled with nuts or truffle mixtures.

Chocolate shells: Large shells make attractive containers for fruit or ice cream and small ones can be used as decorations for cakes and desserts. Cover scallop or other shells with clingfilm. Brush on a thin, even layer of chocolate. Leave until set, then brush on a second layer. When completely hard, carefully peel away the clingfilm.

Piped chocolate: For piping chocolate, use a piping bag fitted with a fine writing nozzle or a greaseproof paper piping bag. Alternatively, use a small polythene food bag and pipe the chocolate straight from the bag (see page 10). A simple way of achieving a professional finish is to pipe melted chocolate directly on to a cake or dessert. It may be piped as writing or as a pattern. The easiest method is to drizzle randomly. To create a feather

design on a cake, cover the top of a cake with glacé icing and immediately pipe on a spiral of melted chocolate, keeping the rings evenly spaced. Draw the tip of a knife from the edge of the cake to the centre, dividing the topping into quarters, then draw the knife from the centre to the edge between these lines to create a feathered effect.

Piped decorations: Draw the outline of the shape on to non-stick baking paper. Pour melted chocolate into a greaseproof paper piping bag. Leave for a few seconds to cool and thicken slightly, then snip off the end of the bag and pipe the chocolate around the drawn outlines. Leave to set, then carefully peel away the paper.

Lacy decorations: Wrap non-stick baking paper around a rolling pin and drizzle on the chocolate in geometric or swirling patterns with a piping bag. Do not make them too thin or they will break. When they are set, remove them carefully from the rolling pin.

Lacy chocolate cups: Turn a bun tin upside down and cover with clingfilm, pressing it down in between the cups. Pipe a circle around the top and bottom edges of the cups, then pipe a trellis pattern over each cup. When set, remove the cups from the tin.

ready-made decorations

If you don't have the time to make your own chocolate decorations, there is a wide selection of ready-made products available. You don't even have to go to specialist shops to find them, as most supermarkets stock a good range. Some will be found in the home-baking section,

while others are from the confectionery section. It is always a good idea to keep a few of these products in store, so that you can instantly enhance the appearance of your cakes and desserts when time is short.

Chocolate chips: These are widely available in plain, milk and white varieties. Chocolate chips can be added to cakes and biscuits and will retain their shape when cooked, or they can be used as simple cake decorations. They melt quickly and easily as an alternative to chocolate bars in cooking.

Chocolate buttons: These are very useful as decorations on children's cakes.

Chocolate flake bars: Flakes make an attractive decoration for cakes, drinks and ice cream. When crumbled, they make an excellent alternative to grated chocolate. Available in milk and white chocolate.

Chocolate vermicelli: Real chocolate vermicelli is not widely available, but the chocolate-coated sugar strands more usually sold as vermicelli are convenient for coating the top and sides of cakes or for sprinkling on ice cream. They can also be used for coating chocolate truffles.

Chocolate leaves: These always look effective on either cakes or desserts.

Chocolate cups and shells: These are available in a variety of sizes and make attractive containers for fruit, ice cream and mousse mixtures.

basic recipes

rich shortcrust pastry

makes: 1 x 20-cm/8-inch flan case
preparation time: 10 minutes, plus
1 hour 30 minutes chilling

175 g/6 oz plain flour, plus extra
for dusting
100 g/3½ oz butter, diced
1 tbsp golden caster sugar
1 egg yolk, beaten with 1 tbsp water

1 Sift the flour into a large bowl.
Add the butter and rub it in with
your fingertips until the mixture resembles
fine breadcrumbs, then stir in the caster
sugar. Stir in the beaten egg yolk.

2 Knead lightly to form a firm dough.
Cover with clingfilm and leave to chill
in the refrigerator for 1 hour 30 minutes.

3 Roll out the dough on to a lightly
floured work surface and use to
line a 20-cm/8-inch flan tin. Proceed as in
main recipe.

extra-rich shortcrust pastry

makes: 8 x 10-cm/4-inch tartlet cases
preparation time: 10 minutes,
plus 1 hour chilling

250 g/9 oz plain flour, plus extra
for dusting
pinch of salt
100 g/3½ oz butter
115 g/4 oz icing sugar
1 large egg, plus 2 large egg yolks

1 Sift the flour and salt into a large
bowl. Make a well in the centre
and add the butter, sugar, egg and yolks.
Using your fingertips, mix the ingredients
in the well into a paste, then gradually
incorporate the flour to make a soft dough.

2 Quickly and lightly knead the
dough, then shape into a ball, wrap
in clingfilm and chill in the refrigerator for
1 hour. Proceed as in main recipe.

basic chocolate pastry

makes: 1 x 23-cm/9-inch flan case
preparation time: 10 minutes, plus
15 minutes chilling

225 g/8 oz plain flour, plus extra
for dusting
2 tbsp cocoa powder
150 g/5½ oz butter
2 tbsp caster sugar
1–2 tbsp cold water

1 Sift the flour and cocoa powder
into a large bowl. Add the butter
and rub it in with your fingertips until the
mixture resembles fine breadcrumbs. Stir
in the caster sugar and enough cold water
to mix to a soft dough.

2 Cover with clingfilm and leave
to chill in the refrigerator for
15 minutes.

3 Roll out the dough on a lightly
floured work surface and use to
line a 23-cm/9-inch loose-bottomed flan
tin. Proceed as in main recipe.

rich chocolate pastry

makes: 1 x 20-cm/8-inch deep
flan case
preparation time: 10 minutes,
plus 30 minutes chilling

4 tbsp cocoa powder
200 g/7 oz plain flour, plus extra
for dusting
100 g/3½ oz softened butter
4 tbsp caster sugar
2 egg yolks
few drops of vanilla essence
1–2 tbsp cold water

1 Sift the cocoa powder and flour
into a large bowl. Add the butter
and rub it in with your fingertips until the
mixture resembles fine breadcrumbs. Stir
in the caster sugar. Add the egg yolks,
vanilla essence and enough water to mix
to a dough.

2 Roll out the dough on a lightly
floured work surface and use it
to line a deep 20-cm/8-inch flan or cake
tin. Leave to chill in the refrigerator for
30 minutes. Proceed as in main recipe.

chocolate sauce

serves: 4
preparation time: 10 minutes

85 g/3 oz plain chocolate
150 ml/5 fl oz single cream

1 Break the chocolate into small
pieces and place in a heavy-based
saucepan with the cream. Heat gently,
stirring constantly, until a smooth sauce
is formed.

2 Transfer to a heatproof jug
and serve warm.

variation

If you like, you can also add
1 tablespoon of brandy to the
chocolate and cream.

ices & cold desserts

An attractively presented, delicious dessert makes a memorable finale to any meal. Indeed, for many people, it's the highlight of the whole event! The beauty of ices and cold desserts is that they can be made in advance, leaving the cook time to concentrate on the rest of the meal without any last-minute panics in the kitchen. Ice creams and frozen desserts are the most versatile of all, as they can be stored in the freezer and are ready to be produced even if an unexpected guest arrives.

The recipes here range from simple ideas, such as Chocolate Coeurs à la Crème (see page 34) or Chocolate & Orange Pots (see page 45), to the more elaborate for a special occasion, such as Double Chocolate Ice Cream Bombe (see page 16) or Chestnut & Chocolate Terrine (see page 39). But even some of the more complicated recipes, like Zucotto (see page 32) or Tiramisù (see page 54), can be made well in advance, in several manageable stages. Some of the desserts offer the sophisticated flavours of rich dark chocolate and liqueur, such as Iced Chocolate Soufflés (see page 23), while others, such as Chocolate Chip & Fudge Banana Ice Cream (see page 22), make ideal treats for children.

double chocolate ice cream bombe

cook: 20 mins

**prep: 50 mins, plus
8–10 hrs freezing**

serves 6–8

*An ice cream bombe is a spectacular dessert to serve at a dinner
party, and the combination of white and dark chocolate is a winner.*

---

variation

For a treat, add 2 tablespoons of
brandy in the dark chocolate ice
cream and 2 tablespoons of
Cointreau in the white chocolate.

---

cook's tip

If you do not have a special bombe
mould, use a plastic bowl instead. Line
it with clingfilm to make the bombe
easier to turn out.

INGREDIENTS

DARK CHOCOLATE ICE CREAM

2 eggs

2 egg yolks

115 g/4 oz golden caster sugar

300 ml/10 fl oz single cream

225 g/8 oz plain chocolate, chopped

300 ml/10 fl oz double cream

WHITE CHOCOLATE ICE CREAM

140 g/5 oz white chocolate, chopped

150 ml/5 fl oz milk

55 g/2 oz golden caster sugar

300 ml/10 fl oz double cream

chocolate decorations, to decorate

(see pages 10–12)

1 Place a 1.5-litre/2¾-pint
bombe mould in the
freezer and set the freezer to
rapid freeze. To make the dark
chocolate ice cream, follow
Steps 1 and 2 of the method
for Dark Chocolate Ice Cream
on page 18.

2 Freeze in an ice cream
maker, according to the
manufacturer's instructions.

Alternatively, pour the mixture
into a large freezerproof
container, then cover and
freeze for 2 hours, or until just
frozen. Spoon into a bowl and
beat with a fork to break
down the ice crystals. Return
to the freezer until almost
solid. Line the bombe mould
with the chocolate ice cream
and freeze for 2 hours, or until
the ice cream is firm.

3 To make the white
chocolate ice cream,
place the chocolate and half
the milk in a saucepan and
heat gently until the chocolate
has just melted. Remove from
the heat and stir. Place the
sugar and remaining milk in a
separate saucepan and heat
gently until the sugar has
melted. Leave to cool, then stir
into the cooled chocolate

mixture. Place the cream in a
bowl and whip until lightly
thickened, then fold into the
chocolate mixture. Spoon into
the centre of the bombe, then
cover and freeze for 4 hours, or
until firm. To serve, dip the
base of the mould briefly
into hot water, then carefully
turn out on to a large serving
plate and decorate with the
chocolate decorations.

dark chocolate ice cream

serves 6   **prep: 25 mins, plus 4 hrs** ⟲   **cook: 15 mins**
30 mins freezing/chilling

*This is a serious chocolate ice cream, which appeals more to adult
tastes. However, if you are serving it to children, omit the brandy.*

INGREDIENTS

2 eggs

2 egg yolks

115 g/4 oz golden caster sugar

300 ml/10 fl oz single cream

225 g/8 oz plain chocolate, chopped

300 ml/10 fl oz double cream

4 tbsp brandy

cook's tip

Set the freezer to its coldest setting
about 1 hour before you intend to
freeze the mixture and remember to
return the freezer to its normal
setting afterwards.

1 Place the whole eggs, egg yolks and sugar in a heatproof bowl and beat together until well blended. Place the single cream and chocolate in a saucepan and heat gently until the chocolate has melted, then continue to heat, stirring constantly, until almost boiling. Pour on to the egg mixture, stirring vigorously, then set the bowl over a saucepan of gently simmering water, making sure that the base of the bowl does not touch the water.

2 Cook, stirring constantly, until the mixture lightly coats the back of the spoon. Sieve into a separate bowl and leave to cool. Place the double cream and brandy in a separate bowl and whip until slightly thickened, then fold into the cooled chocolate mixture.

3 Freeze in an ice cream maker, following the manufacturer's instructions. Alternatively, pour the mixture into a large freezerproof container, then cover and freeze for 2 hours, or until just frozen. Spoon into a bowl and beat with a fork to break down the ice crystals. Return to the freezer for 2 hours, or until firm. Transfer the ice cream to the refrigerator 30 minutes before serving. Scoop the ice cream into 4 serving dishes or coffee cups and serve.

marbled chocolate & orange ice cream

cook: 15 mins

prep: 15 mins, plus 10 hrs 30 mins freezing/chilling

serves 6

Swirls of orange-flavoured chocolate run through the white chocolate and not only look attractive but taste delicious too.

cook's tip

To make this into a mint ice cream, use good-quality mint-flavoured plain chocolate instead of the orange-flavoured plain chocolate, if you like.

INGREDIENTS

175 g/6 oz white chocolate

1 tsp cornflour

1 tsp vanilla essence

3 egg yolks

300 ml/10 fl oz milk

450 ml/16 fl oz double cream

115 g/4 oz orange-flavoured plain chocolate, broken into pieces

grated orange rind, to decorate

orange segments, to serve

1 Chop the white chocolate into small pieces and reserve. Place the cornflour, vanilla essence and egg yolks in a heatproof bowl and beat together until well blended. Pour the milk into a large, heavy-based saucepan and bring to the boil over a low heat. Pour over the egg yolk mixture, stirring constantly.

2 Sieve the mixture back into the saucepan and heat gently, stirring, until thickened. Remove from the heat, add the white chocolate pieces and stir until melted. Stir in the cream. Reserve 150 ml/5 fl oz of the mixture and pour the remainder into a large freezerproof container. Cover and freeze for 2 hours, or until beginning to set. Melt the orange-flavoured chocolate (see pages 9–10), stir into the reserved mixture and reserve.

3 Remove the partially frozen ice cream from the freezer and beat with a fork. Place spoonfuls of the orange chocolate mixture over the ice cream and swirl with a knife to give a marbled effect. Freeze for 8 hours, or overnight, until firm. Transfer to the refrigerator 30 minutes before serving. Scoop into individual glasses, decorate with orange rind and serve with a few orange segments.

coconut & white chocolate ice cream

serves 6   **prep: 25 mins, plus 5 hrs 30 mins freezing/chilling** ⏲   **cook: 15 mins** ⏱

Coconut and white chocolate combine to make a smooth, creamy ice cream with an exotic flavour. Perfect for a hot summer's day.

INGREDIENTS

2 eggs

2 egg yolks

115 g/4 oz golden caster sugar

300 ml/10 fl oz single cream

115 g/4 oz white chocolate, chopped

115 g/4 oz creamed coconut, chopped

300 ml/10 fl oz double cream

3 tbsp coconut rum

tropical fruit, such as mango, pineapple or passion fruit, to serve

variation

As an alternative to serving with fruit, this ice cream is also delicious served with a Chocolate Sauce (see page 13) poured over the top.

cook's tip

To make serving the ice cream easier, dip the ice cream scoop briefly in a small bowl of hot water before serving each portion. If you don't have an ice cream scoop, a serving spoon will be just as good.

1 Place the whole eggs, egg yolks and sugar in a heatproof bowl and beat together until well blended. Place the single cream, chocolate and coconut in a saucepan and heat gently until the chocolate has melted, then continue to heat, stirring constantly, until almost boiling. Pour on to the egg mixture, stirring vigorously, then set the bowl over a saucepan of gently simmering water, making sure that the base of the bowl does not touch the water.

2 Heat the mixture, stirring constantly, until it lightly coats the back of the spoon. Sieve into a clean, heatproof bowl and leave to cool. Place the double cream and rum in a separate bowl and whip until slightly thickened, then fold into the cooled chocolate mixture.

3 Freeze in an ice cream maker, following the manufacturer's instructions. Alternatively, pour the mixture into a large freezerproof container, then cover and freeze for 2 hours, or until just frozen. Spoon into a bowl and beat with a fork to break down the ice crystals. Return to the freezer for 3 hours, or until firm. Transfer the ice cream to the refrigerator for 30 minutes before serving. Scoop into small serving bowls and serve with tropical fruit.

chocolate chip & fudge banana ice cream

serves 6　　**prep: 15 mins, plus 6 hrs 15 mins freezing/chilling** ⟳　　**cook: 0 mins** ⏲

This indulgent ice cream is equally popular with both adults and children and makes a wonderful midweek dessert.

INGREDIENTS

4 ripe bananas

juice of ½ lemon

200 g/7 oz golden caster sugar

500 ml/18 fl oz whipping cream

100 g/3½ oz plain chocolate chips

100 g/3½ oz fudge, cut into small pieces, plus extra to decorate

cook's tip

Choose bananas that are ripe but not brown. It is important to add lemon juice as the juice helps to prevent the bananas turning brown.

1 Peel the bananas and chop them roughly, then place in a food processor with the lemon juice and sugar. Process until well chopped, then pour in the cream and process again until well blended.

2 Freeze in an ice cream maker, following the manufacturer's instructions, adding the chocolate chips and fudge just before the ice cream is ready. Alternatively, pour the mixture into a large freezerproof container, then cover and freeze for 2 hours, or until just frozen. Spoon into a bowl and beat with a fork to break down the ice crystals. Return the ice cream to the freezer for a further 2 hours, or until almost firm. Remove from the freezer, beat again and stir in the chocolate chips and fudge. Return to the freezer for a further 2 hours, or until firm.

3 Transfer the ice cream to the refrigerator 15 minutes before serving. Scoop into small bowls and decorate with extra fudge pieces. Serve.

iced chocolate soufflés

🕐 cook: 5 mins   🕐 prep: 30 mins, plus 8 hrs freezing   **serves 6**

Individual iced soufflés look very special, and make serving easier too! For an elegant presentation, decorate with chocolate curls.

cook's tip

When whisking egg whites, make sure the bowl is dry, spotlessly clean and free from any grease, otherwise the whites will not hold their shape.

INGREDIENTS

100 g/3½ oz plain chocolate, chopped

1 tbsp instant coffee powder

2 tbsp water

4 eggs, separated

115 g/4 oz icing sugar, sifted

225 ml/8 fl oz double cream

2 tbsp Tia Maria

Chocolate Curls (see page 10),

to decorate

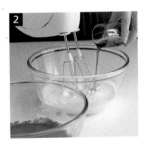

1. Tie a double band of foil tightly around each of 6 ramekin dishes, to stand 2.5 cm/1 inch above the rim. Place the chocolate, coffee powder and water in a small saucepan and heat gently until melted. Leave to cool slightly.

2. Place the egg yolks and icing sugar in a bowl. Beat with an electric whisk until thick and light. Whisk in the melted chocolate mixture. Place the cream and Tia Maria in a separate bowl and whip until thick. Reserve.

3. Whisk the egg whites in a separate, clean, greasefree bowl until stiff but not dry. Stir 1 tablespoon of the whisked egg whites into the chocolate mixture, then gently fold in the remaining egg whites with the cream. Pour into the ramekins and freeze for 8 hours, or overnight. Remove the foil carefully. Decorate the soufflés with chocolate curls and serve.

italian chocolate christmas pudding

cook: 5 mins   **prep: 15 mins, plus 8 hrs chilling**   **serves 10**

This pudding is a wonderful alternative for anyone who dislikes a traditional Christmas pudding, but there is absolutely no reason why it should be served only at Christmas!

variation

For a change, substitute the amaretti biscuits with crushed digestive biscuits and replace the Amaretto liqueur with the same amount of brandy.

cook's tip

As this pudding is very rich, it should be cut into very thin slices. To make it easier to slice, dip a sharp knife into hot water and wipe away any excess water before slicing.

INGREDIENTS

butter, for greasing
115 g/4 oz mixed glacé fruit, chopped
55 g/2 oz raisins
grated rind of ½ orange
3 tbsp orange juice
3 tbsp single cream
350 g/12 oz plain chocolate, chopped
115 g/4 oz cream cheese
115 g/4 oz amaretti biscuits, broken into rough pieces

TO SERVE
125 ml/4 fl oz whipping cream
2 tbsp Amaretto liqueur
25 g/1 oz plain chocolate, grated

1 Grease an 850-ml/ 1½-pint pudding basin with butter. Place the glacé fruit, raisins, orange rind and juice in a bowl and mix together. Place the single cream and chocolate in a saucepan and heat gently until the chocolate has melted. Stir until smooth, then stir in the fruit mixture. Leave to cool.

2 Place the cream cheese and a little of the chocolate mixture in a large bowl and beat together until smooth, then stir in the remaining chocolate mixture. Stir in the broken amaretti biscuits. Pour into the prepared basin, cover with clingfilm and leave to chill in the refrigerator overnight.

3 To serve, turn the pudding out on to a chilled serving plate. Pour the whipping cream into a bowl and add the Amaretto liqueur. Whip lightly until slightly thickened. Pour some of the cream over the pudding and sprinkle grated chocolate over the top. Serve with the remaining cream.

chocolate sorbet

serves 6   prep: 15 mins, plus 🕒 9 hrs freezing/chilling   cook: 10 mins 🕒

This chocolate sorbet makes a light and refreshing yet luxurious end to any meal. It is especially good served with some crisp biscuits and freshly brewed coffee.

INGREDIENTS

55 g/2 oz cocoa powder

150 g/5½ oz golden caster sugar

2 tsp instant coffee granules

500 ml/18 fl oz water

crisp biscuits, to serve

cook's tip

Making the sorbet in an ice cream maker will give the best results. If you do not have one, beat the sorbet frequently while it is freezing to help make it light and smooth.

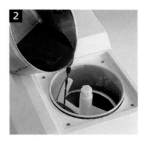

1 Sift the cocoa powder into a small, heavy-based saucepan and add the caster sugar, coffee granules and a little of the water. Using a wooden spoon, mix together to form a thin paste, then gradually stir in the remaining water. Bring the mixture to the boil over a low heat and simmer gently for 8 minutes, stirring frequently.

2 Remove the saucepan from the heat and leave to cool. Transfer the mixture to a bowl, cover with clingfilm and place in the refrigerator until well chilled. Freeze in an ice cream maker, following the manufacturer's instructions. Alternatively, pour the mixture into a large freezerproof container, then cover and freeze for 2 hours. Remove the sorbet from the freezer and beat with a fork to break down the ice crystals. Freeze for a further 6 hours, beating the sorbet every 2 hours.

3 Transfer the sorbet to the refrigerator 30 minutes before serving. Scoop into 6 serving bowls and serve with crisp biscuits.

chocolate kulfi

⏱ **cook: 20 mins**   ⏱ **prep: 1 hr, plus 10 hrs freezing**   **serves 6**

Kulfi is a delicately spiced Indian ice cream traditionally made in tube-shaped terracotta containers. Although chocolate is not an authentic ingredient, it makes this ice cream even more of a treat.

cook's tip

Use a wide, heavy-based saucepan for reducing the milk to allow plenty of room for the liquid to bubble up. This will also help to speed up the evaporation.

INGREDIENTS

2 litres/3½ pints creamy milk

12 whole cardamom pods

85 g/3 oz golden caster sugar

100 g/3½ oz plain chocolate, chopped

10 g/¼ oz blanched almonds, chopped

25 g/1 oz shelled unsalted pistachio nuts, chopped

1 Place the milk and cardamom pods in a large, heavy-based saucepan. Bring to the boil over a low heat, then simmer vigorously until reduced to one-third of its original amount.

2 Sieve the milk into a heatproof bowl, discarding the cardamom pods, then stir in the sugar and chocolate until melted. Add the almonds and half the pistachio nuts, then leave to cool. Pour the mixture into a large freezerproof container, then cover and freeze for 2 hours, or until almost firm, stirring every 30 minutes.

3 Pack the ice cream into 6 yogurt pots or dariole moulds, cover with clingfilm and freeze for 8 hours, or until completely solid. To serve, dip the base of the moulds briefly into hot water, then turn out on to dessert plates. Sprinkle over the remaining pistachio nuts to decorate and serve.

chocolate banana sundae

serves 4   **prep: 15 mins** ⏱   **cook: 5 mins** 🍲

A banana split in a glass! Choose the best-quality vanilla ice cream you can find, or, better still, if you have time make your own.

INGREDIENTS

SAUCE

55 g/2 oz plain chocolate

4 tbsp golden syrup

1 tbsp butter

1 tbsp brandy or rum (optional)

SUNDAE

4 bananas

150 ml/5 fl oz double cream

8–12 scoops of good-quality vanilla ice cream

75 g/2¾ oz flaked or chopped almonds, toasted

grated or flaked chocolate, for sprinkling

4 fan wafer biscuits, to serve

---

variation

For a traditional banana split, halve the bananas lengthways and place on a plate with 2 scoops of ice cream. Top with cream, nuts and chocolate sauce.

---

cook's tip

When melting chocolate in a heatproof bowl set over a saucepan of simmering water, make sure that the bowl does not touch the water.

1 To make the sauce, break the chocolate into small pieces and place in a heatproof bowl with the syrup and butter. Place the bowl over a saucepan of hot water and heat until melted, stirring constantly, until well blended. Remove from the heat and stir in the brandy or rum, if using.

2 Peel and slice the bananas. Place the cream in a large bowl and whip until just holding its shape. Place a scoop of ice cream in the bottom of 4 tall sundae dishes, then top with slices of banana, some sauce, a spoonful of cream and a generous sprinkling of nuts.

3 Repeat the layers, finishing with a generous spoonful of cream, sprinkled with nuts and a little grated chocolate. Serve with fan wafer biscuits.

baked chocolate alaska

⏲ **cook: 12 mins**   ⏱ **prep: 50 mins**   **serves 4**

A very cool dessert that leaves the cook completely unflustered – assemble it in advance and just freeze until required.

variation

Try adding a layer of mixed canned fruit on top of the sponge, then top with the ice cream and meringue. Proceed as in main recipe.

cook's tip

This dessert is delicious served with a blackcurrant coulis. Cook a few blackcurrants in a little orange juice until soft, purée and push through a sieve, then sweeten to taste with a little icing sugar.

INGREDIENTS

butter, for greasing

2 eggs

4 tbsp caster sugar

5 tbsp plain flour

2 tbsp cocoa powder

3 egg whites

150 g/5½ oz caster sugar

1 litre/1¾ pints good-quality chocolate ice cream

1 Preheat the oven to 220°C/425°F/Gas Mark 7. Grease an 18-cm/7-inch round cake tin with butter and line the base with baking paper.

2 Whisk the eggs and the 4 tablespoons of sugar in a bowl until very thick and pale. Sift the flour and cocoa powder together and fold in.

3 Pour into the prepared tin and bake in the preheated oven for 7 minutes, or until springy to the touch. Transfer to a wire rack to cool.

4 Whisk the egg whites in a spotlessly clean, greasefree bowl until soft peaks form. Gradually add the sugar, whisking, until you have a thick, glossy meringue.

5 Place the sponge on a large baking tray and pile the ice cream in the centre in a heaped dome.

6 Pipe or spread the meringue over the ice cream, making sure that the ice cream is completely enclosed. (At this point the dessert can be frozen, if you like.)

7 Return to the oven for 5 minutes, or until the meringue is just golden. Serve immediately.

zucotto

serves 6

prep: 30 mins, plus
7–9 hrs chilling/cooling

cook: 15–20 mins

Zucotto is a traditional Italian dessert that combines those natural partners, plain chocolate and black cherries.

INGREDIENTS

115 g/4 oz soft margarine, plus
extra for greasing
100 g/3½ oz self-raising flour
2 tbsp cocoa powder
½ tsp baking powder
115 g/4 oz golden caster sugar
2 eggs, beaten
3 tbsp brandy
2 tbsp kirsch

FILLING
300 ml/10 fl oz double cream
25 g/1 oz icing sugar, sifted
55 g/2 oz toasted almonds, chopped
225 g/8 oz black cherries, stoned
55 g/2 oz plain chocolate,
finely chopped

TO DECORATE
1 tbsp cocoa powder
1 tbsp icing sugar
fresh cherries

variation

If fresh cherries are not available,
use drained canned cherries instead.
Replace the kirsch with an almond-
flavoured liqueur, such as Amaretto.

cook's tip

If the zucotto is thoroughly chilled
beforehand it can be left unmoulded
for a couple of hours at the table,
making it ideal to serve as part of a
buffet lunch.

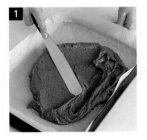

1 Preheat the oven to 190°C/375°F/Gas Mark 5. Grease a 30 x 23-cm/12 x 9-inch Swiss roll tin with margarine and line with baking paper. Sift the flour, cocoa and baking powder into a bowl. Add the sugar, margarine and eggs. Beat together until well mixed, then spoon into the prepared tin. Bake in the preheated oven for 15–20 minutes, or

until well risen and firm to the touch. Leave in the tin for 5 minutes, then turn out on to a wire rack to cool.

2 Using the rim of a 1.2-litre/2-pint pudding basin as a guide, cut a round from the cake and reserve. Line the basin with clingfilm. Use the remaining cake, cutting it as necessary, to line the basin.

Place the brandy and kirsch in a small bowl and mix together. Sprinkle over the cake, including the reserved round.

3 To make the filling, pour the cream into a separate bowl and add the icing sugar. Whip until thick, then fold in the almonds, cherries and chocolate. Fill the sponge mould with the cream

mixture and press the cake round on top. Cover with a plate and a weight, and leave to chill in the refrigerator for 6–8 hours, or overnight. When ready to serve, turn the zucotto out on to a serving plate. Decorate with cocoa powder and icing sugar, sifted over in alternating segments, and a few fresh cherries.

chocolate coeurs à la crème

cook: 0 mins   **prep: 20 mins, plus 8 hrs chilling**   **serves 8**

This is a delicious adaptation of a classic French dessert, traditionally made in pierced heart-shaped porcelain moulds.

variation

Other types of fresh berries would work equally well as a coulis. Try blackcurrants or blackberries, if they are in season.

cook's tip

As in this recipe, substitute pierced yogurt pots in place of the authentic porcelain moulds. Top with halved fresh strawberries for the *coeur* or heart shape.

INGREDIENTS

225 g/8 oz ricotta cheese
55 g/2 oz icing sugar, sifted
300 ml/10 fl oz double cream
1 tsp vanilla essence
55 g/2 oz plain chocolate, grated
2 egg whites

COULIS

225 g/8 oz fresh raspberries
icing sugar, to taste

TO DECORATE

fresh strawberries, halved
fresh raspberries

1 Line 8 individual moulds with muslin. Rub the ricotta cheese through a sieve into a bowl. Add the icing sugar, cream and vanilla essence and beat together thoroughly. Stir in the grated chocolate. Place the egg whites in a separate clean bowl and whisk until stiff but not dry. Gently fold into the cheese mixture.

2 Spoon the mixture into the prepared moulds. Stand the moulds on a tray or dish and leave in the refrigerator to drain for 8 hours, or overnight – the muslin will absorb most of the liquid.

3 To make the raspberry coulis, place the raspberries in a food processor and process to a purée. Press

the purée through a sieve into a bowl and add icing sugar, to taste. To serve, turn each dessert out on to a serving plate and pour the raspberry coulis around. Decorate with halved strawberries and raspberries, then serve.

chocolate rum creams

prep: 10 mins, plus ⏱
2 hrs cooling/chilling

cook: 5 mins ⏱

This dessert requires no cooking apart from warming the cream, and is extremely easy to make. It is particularly good served with crisp biscuits and makes a superb finale to a dinner party menu.

INGREDIENTS

100 g/3½ oz plain chocolate, broken
into pieces
150 ml/5 fl oz single cream
300 ml/10 fl oz whipping cream
1 tbsp icing sugar, sifted
2 tbsp white rum
Chocolate Curls (see page 10),
to decorate

cook's tip

This dessert looks particularly attractive served in matching tall glasses. You can also use coffee cups, or ordinary dessert dishes would work just as well.

1 Place the chocolate and single cream in a small, heavy-based saucepan and heat very gently until the chocolate has melted. Stir until smooth, then remove from the heat and leave to cool. Pour the whipping cream into a large bowl and, using an electric whisk, whip until thick but not stiff.

2 Carefully whisk the cooled sugar, rum and chocolate mixture into the whipped cream. Take care not to overwhisk.

3 Spoon the mixture into 6 serving dishes or glasses, cover with clingfilm and leave to chill in the refrigerator for 1–2 hours.

4 Make the Chocolate Curls and sprinkle them carefully over the creams before serving.

chocolate & strawberry brûlées

⏱ **cook: 8 mins**   ⏱ **prep: 15 mins, plus 2 hrs 30 mins freezing/thawing**   **serves 6**

Fresh fruit covered with a delicious chocolate cream and crunchy caramelized topping couldn't be easier to make, yet it is impressive enough to serve at any dinner party.

cook's tip

Freezing the brûlées before grilling ensures that the cream will not bubble up through the sugar, but if short of time, it is not necessary to freeze them. You can caramelize the sugar with a culinary blowtorch.

INGREDIENTS

250 g/9 oz fresh strawberries, washed and hulled

2 tbsp fruit liqueur, such as kirsch or crème de cassis

450 ml/16 fl oz double cream

115 g/4 oz plain chocolate, melted and cooled (see pages 9–10)

115 g/4 oz demerara sugar

TO DECORATE

fresh strawberries

fresh mint leaves

1 | Cut the strawberries into halves or quarters, depending on their size, and divide among 6 ramekin dishes. Sprinkle with the fruit liqueur.

2 | Pour the cream into a bowl and whip until it is just holding its shape. Add the cooled chocolate and continue whipping until the cream is thick. Spread over the strawberries. Cover and place in the freezer for 2 hours, or until the cream is frozen.

3 | Preheat the grill to high. Sprinkle the sugar thickly over the cream, then place under the hot grill and cook until the sugar has melted and caramelized. Leave the brûlées to stand for 30 minutes, or until the fruit and cream have thawed. Serve decorated with a few fresh strawberries and mint leaves.

black & white pudding

serves 4–6

prep: 30 mins, plus 30 mins cooling

cook: 45 mins

This rich dessert is a cross between a steamed pudding and a soufflé. It makes an extravagant treat whatever the occasion.

INGREDIENTS

oil, for brushing

115 g/4 oz unsalted butter

115 g/4 oz golden caster sugar

½ tsp ground cardamom seeds

4 eggs, separated

115 g/4 oz plain chocolate, melted and cooled (see pages 9–10)

1 tbsp rum

150 ml/5 fl oz double cream

50 ml/2 fl oz crème fraîche

variation

Instead of the cream and crème fraîche, serve with fresh summer berries, such as raspberries and blackcurrants, and vanilla ice cream.

1 Lightly brush an 850-ml/1½-pint pudding basin with oil. Place the butter, sugar and cardamom in a bowl and beat together until light and thick. Gradually beat in the egg yolks. Carefully stir in the cooled chocolate and the rum. Place the egg whites in a separate spotlessly clean, greasefree bowl and whisk until stiff but not dry. Stir 1 tablespoon of the whisked egg whites into the chocolate mixture, then carefully fold in the remainder.

2 Turn the mixture into the prepared basin. Cover with oiled baking paper and foil and tie securely with string. Place the bowl in a large, heavy-based saucepan and pour in enough boiling water to come one-third of the way up the side of the basin. Cover the saucepan and simmer gently for 45 minutes.

3 Leave the pudding in the basin until cold, then turn out on to a serving dish. Whip the cream and crème fraîche together until thick. Cover the pudding with the cream or serve separately.

chestnut & chocolate terrine

🕐 **cook: 5 mins**   🕐 **prep: 30 mins, plus 8 hrs chilling**   **serves 6**

Chestnut and chocolate is an all-time classic combination and it is experienced at its best in this delicious layered terrine.

variation
You can substitute Marsala wine or dry sherry for the rum, if you would prefer a different flavour.

INGREDIENTS

200 ml/7 fl oz double cream

115 g/4 oz plain chocolate, melted and cooled (see pages 9–10)

100 ml/3½ fl oz rum

1 packet rectangular, plain, sweet biscuits, such as Nice

225 g/8 oz canned sweetened chestnut purée

cocoa powder, for dusting

icing sugar, to decorate

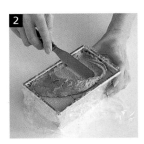

1 Line a 450-g/1-lb loaf tin with clingfilm. Place the cream in a bowl and whip lightly until soft peaks form. Using a spatula, fold in the cooled chocolate.

2 Place the rum in a shallow dish. Lightly dip 4 biscuits into the rum and arrange on the base of the tin. Repeat with 4 more biscuits.

Spread half the chocolate cream over the biscuits. Make another layer of 8 biscuits dipped in rum and spread over the chestnut purée, followed by another layer of biscuits. Spread over the remaining chocolate cream and top with a final layer of biscuits. Cover with clingfilm and leave to chill in the refrigerator for 8 hours, or preferably overnight.

3 Turn the terrine out on to a large serving dish. Dust with cocoa powder. Cut strips of paper and place these randomly on top of the terrine. Sift over icing sugar. Carefully remove the paper.
To serve, dip a sharp knife in hot water, dry it, and use it to cut the terrine into slices.

chocolate & hazelnut parfait

 cook: 10 mins   prep: 30 mins, plus 8 hrs 20 mins cooling/freezing   serves 6

Richly flavoured, moulded ice creams make a scrumptious summertime dessert for all the family.

variation

Replace the blanched hazelnuts with other types of nuts, such as macadamias, almonds or Brazil nuts, if you prefer.

cook's tip

Melt chocolate slowly and gradually as it easily burns and becomes unusable. As soon as the chocolate has melted, remove the saucepan from the heat.

INGREDIENTS

175 g/6 oz blanched hazelnuts

175 g/6 oz plain chocolate, broken into small pieces

600 ml/1 pint double cream

3 eggs, separated

250 g/9 oz icing sugar

1 tbsp cocoa powder, for dusting

6 small fresh mint sprigs, to decorate

wafer biscuits, to serve

1 Preheat the grill to medium. Spread out the hazelnuts on a baking tray and toast under the grill for 5 minutes until golden. Cool.

2 Place the chocolate in a heatproof bowl and set over a pan of simmering water until melted. Cool. Place the hazelnuts in a food processor and process until ground.

3 Whisk the cream until stiff, then fold in the hazelnuts and reserve. Beat the egg yolks with 3 tablespoons of the sugar for 10 minutes, or until pale and thick.

4 Whisk the egg whites in a clean, greasefree bowl until soft peaks form. Whisk in the remaining sugar, a little at a time, until the whites are stiff and glossy. Stir the cooled chocolate into the egg yolk mixture, then fold in the cream. Fold in the egg whites. Divide the mixture between 6 freezerproof moulds, cover with clingfilm and freeze for at least 8 hours until firm.

5 Transfer the parfaits to the refrigerator 10 minutes before serving to soften slightly. Turn out on to 6 serving plates, dust the tops lightly with cocoa powder, decorate with mint sprigs and serve with wafers.

chocolate terrine with orange cream

serves 10–12

prep: 30 mins, plus 3 hrs chilling

cook: 10 mins

Contrasting bands of white, milk and dark chocolate look stunning when this terrine is sliced and surrounded with orange cream.

INGREDIENTS

6 tbsp water

3 tsp powdered gelatine

115 g/4 oz each of milk, white and plain chocolate, broken into pieces

450 ml/16 fl oz whipping cream

6 eggs, separated

75 g/2¾ oz caster sugar

ORANGE CREAM

25 g/1 oz caster sugar

1 tbsp cornflour

2 egg yolks

150 ml/5 fl oz milk

150 ml/5 fl oz double cream

grated rind of 1 orange

1 tbsp Cointreau or orange juice (optional)

TO DECORATE

150 ml/5 fl oz double cream, whipped

chocolate-covered coffee beans

orange zest

variation

As an alternative to the orange cream, simply serve the terrine with some pouring cream, if you like.

cook's tip

When lining a terrine or loaf tin with clingfilm, make sure that there is a generous overhang, so you can use it to cover the top before freezing.

1 Line a 1.2-litre/2-pint terrine or loaf tin with clingfilm. To make the milk chocolate mousse, place 2 tablespoons of the water in a heatproof bowl. Sprinkle on 1 teaspoon of gelatine and leave for 5 minutes. Set the bowl over a pan of simmering water until the gelatine has dissolved. Cool. Melt the milk chocolate (see pages 9–10)

and cool. Whip one-third of the cream until thick. Whisk 2 of the egg whites in a bowl until stiff but not dry. Whisk 2 of the egg yolks and one-third of the sugar in a separate bowl until thick. Stir in the chocolate, dissolved gelatine and whipped cream. Fold in the whisked egg whites. Pour into the tin. Cover and freeze for 20 minutes, or until set.

2 Make the white chocolate mousse in the same way, pour over the milk chocolate mousse and freeze. Make the plain chocolate mousse and pour on top. Chill for 2 hours, until set.

3 To make the orange cream, stir the sugar, cornflour and egg yolks together until smooth. Heat

the milk, cream and orange rind in a saucepan until almost boiling, then pour over the egg mixture, whisking. Sieve back into the pan and heat until thick. Cover and cool. Stir in the Cointreau. The cream should be runny; if not, stir in a little orange juice. Turn out the terrine. Decorate with cream, coffee beans and orange zest. Serve with the orange cream.

white chocolate mousse

serves 6 **prep: 15 mins, plus 8 hrs chilling** **cook: 8 mins**

White chocolate makes a sweet and creamy mousse, and fragrant rosewater adds an interesting flavour.

INGREDIENTS

250 g/9 oz white chocolate, broken into pieces

100 ml/3½ fl oz milk

300 ml/10 fl oz double cream

1 tsp rosewater

2 egg whites

115 g/4 oz plain chocolate, broken into pieces

crystallized rose petals, to decorate

1 Place the white chocolate and milk in a saucepan and heat gently until the chocolate has melted, then stir. Transfer to a large bowl and leave to cool.

2 Place the cream and rosewater in a separate bowl and whip until soft peaks form. Whisk the egg whites in a separate spotlessly clean, greasefree bowl until stiff but not dry. Gently fold the whipped cream into the chocolate, then fold in the egg whites. Spoon the mixture into 6 small dishes or glasses, cover with clingfilm and chill in the refrigerator for 8 hours, or overnight, to set.

3 Melt the plain chocolate (see pages 9–10) and leave to cool, then pour evenly over the mousses. Leave until the chocolate has hardened, then decorate with rose petals and serve.

chocolate & orange pots

cook: 5 mins **prep: 15 mins, plus 1 hr chilling** **serves 8**

These little pots of rich chocolate cream will satisfy the most serious chocolate-lovers. They look superb served in matching coffee cups.

cook's tip

Leave the chocolate pots to chill in the refrigerator for no more than 2 hours, otherwise the mixture becomes too firmly set in the ramekin dishes or cups.

INGREDIENTS

200 g/7 oz plain chocolate, broken into pieces

grated rind of 1 orange

300 ml/10 fl oz double cream

140 g/5 oz golden caster sugar

3 tbsp Cointreau

3 large egg whites

fine strips of orange rind, to decorate

crisp biscuits, to serve

1 Melt the chocolate (see pages 9–10) and stir in the orange rind. Place the cream in a bowl with 100 g/3½ oz of the sugar and the Cointreau and whip until thick.

2 Place the egg whites in a separate spotlessly clean, greasefree bowl and whisk until soft peaks form, then gradually whisk in the remaining sugar until stiff but not dry. Fold the melted chocolate into the cream, then beat in a spoonful of the whisked egg whites. Gently fold in the remaining egg whites until thoroughly mixed.

3 Spoon the mixture into 8 small ramekin dishes or demi-tasse coffee cups. Cover and leave to chill in the refrigerator for 1 hour, then decorate with a few strips of orange rind before serving with crisp biscuits.

oeufs à la neige au chocolat

⏲ **cook: 15–20 mins**   ⏱ **prep: 15 mins, plus 2 hrs chilling**   **serves 6**

In this dessert, poached meringues float on a richly flavoured chocolate custard like little snowballs.

---

variation

You can also drizzle caramel over the top. Dissolve 2 tablespoons of sugar in 3 tablespoons of water in a saucepan and boil until a caramel has formed.

---

cook's tip

Cook the custard over a low heat and do not let it boil as it will curdle and separate. If it does begin to curdle, remove the saucepan from the heat and sieve the custard into a cold bowl.

INGREDIENTS

600 ml/1 pint milk

1 tsp vanilla essence

175 g/6 oz caster sugar

2 egg whites

cocoa powder, for dusting

CUSTARD

4 tbsp caster sugar

3 tbsp cocoa powder

4 egg yolks

1 Place the milk, vanilla essence and 5 tablespoons of the sugar in a heavy-based saucepan and stir over a low heat until the sugar has dissolved. Simmer gently.

2 Whisk the egg whites in a spotlessly clean, greasefree bowl until stiff peaks form. Whisk in 2 teaspoons of the remaining sugar and continue to whisk until glossy. Gently fold in the rest of the sugar.

3 Drop large spoonfuls of the meringue mixture on to the simmering milk mixture and cook, stirring once, for 4–5 minutes, or until the meringues are firm. Remove with a slotted spoon and leave to drain on kitchen paper. Poach the remaining meringues in the same way, then reserve the milk mixture.

4 To make the custard, mix the sugar, cocoa powder and egg yolks in the top of a double boiler or in a heatproof bowl. Gradually whisk in the reserved milk mixture. Place over barely simmering water and cook for 5–10 minutes, whisking constantly, until thickened. Remove from the heat and cool slightly. Divide the chocolate custard between 6 serving glasses and top with the meringues. Cover and leave to chill in the refrigerator for at least 2 hours. When ready to serve, dust the tops of the meringues with cocoa powder.

chocolate mint swirl

serves 6　　prep: 15 mins, plus 🕐 30 mins cooling/setting　　cook: 5 mins ⏲

The classic combination of chocolate and mint flavours makes an attractive dessert for all kinds of special occasions.

INGREDIENTS

300 ml/10 fl oz double cream

150 ml/5 fl oz creamy fromage frais

2 tbsp icing sugar

1 tbsp crème de menthe

175 g/6 oz plain chocolate

55 g/2 oz plain chocolate, to decorate

variation

For a chocolate orange swirl, replace the crème de menthe with the same amount of Cointreau.

cook's tip

Pipe the patterns freehand or draw patterns on to baking paper first, turn the paper over and pipe the chocolate, carefully following the drawn outline.

1 Place the cream in a large bowl and whip until soft peaks form.

2 Fold in the fromage frais and sugar, then place one-third of the mixture in a smaller bowl. Stir the crème de menthe into the small bowl. Melt the chocolate (see pages 9–10) and stir it into the remaining mixture.

3 Place alternate spoonfuls of the 2 mixtures into serving glasses, then swirl the mixture together to give a decorative effect. Leave to cool, then chill in the refrigerator until required.

4 To make the piped chocolate decorations, melt a small amount of chocolate (see pages 9–10) and place in a paper piping bag. Place a sheet of baking paper on a board and pipe squiggles, stars or flower shapes with the melted chocolate. Alternatively, pipe decorations on to a long strip of baking paper, then place the strip over a rolling pin, securing with sticky tape. Leave to set, then remove from the baking paper.

5 Decorate each dessert with piped chocolate decorations and serve. The desserts can be decorated and chilled in the refrigerator, if you like.

coffee panna cotta with chocolate sauce

cook: 10 mins **prep: 25 mins, plus 8 hrs chilling** **serves 6**

Panna cotta literally means 'cooked cream'. Flavouring it with coffee and serving it with a chocolate sauce adds a new look to this popular Italian dessert.

variation

For a special occasion, use heart-shaped moulds lined with clingfilm for easy removal. They are available from most kitchen shops.

cook's tip

Individual metal pudding basin moulds are ideal for these desserts – the panna cotta turns out more easily than from china moulds.

INGREDIENTS

oil, for brushing

600 ml/1 pint double cream

1 vanilla pod

55 g/2 oz golden caster sugar

2 tsp instant espresso coffee granules, dissolved in 4 tbsp water

2 tsp powdered gelatine

chocolate-covered coffee beans, to serve

SAUCE

150 ml/5 fl oz single cream

55 g/2 oz plain chocolate, melted (see pages 9–10)

1 Lightly brush 6 x 150-ml/5-fl oz moulds with oil. Place the cream in a saucepan. Split the vanilla pod and scrape the black seeds into the cream. Add the vanilla pod and the sugar, then heat gently until almost boiling. Sieve the cream into a heatproof bowl and reserve. Place the coffee in a small heatproof bowl, sprinkle on the gelatine and leave for 5 minutes, or until spongy. Set the bowl over a saucepan of gently simmering water until the gelatine has dissolved.

2 Stir a little of the reserved cream into the gelatine mixture, then stir the gelatine mixture into the remainder of the cream. Divide the mixture between the prepared moulds and leave to cool, then leave to chill in the refrigerator for 8 hours, or overnight.

3 To make the sauce, place one-quarter of the cream in a bowl and stir in the melted chocolate. Gradually stir in the remaining cream, reserving 1 tablespoon. To serve the panna cotta, dip the base of the moulds briefly into hot water and turn out on to 6 dessert plates. Pour the chocolate cream around. Dot drops of the reserved cream on to the sauce and feather it with a skewer. Decorate with chocolate-covered coffee beans and serve.

mocha creams

cook: 5 mins   **prep: 10 mins, plus 20 mins standing/setting**   **serves 4**

These delicious creamy chocolate- and coffee-flavoured desserts make a perfect end to any dinner party meal.

---

variation

To add a delicious almond flavour to the dessert, replace the coffee-flavoured liqueur with Amaretto, an almond-flavoured liqueur.

cook's tip

Always whip cream in a large bowl as the cream will double in volume. If using an electric mixer, always begin whipping slowly and gradually increase the speed.

INGREDIENTS

225 g/8 oz plain chocolate
1 tbsp instant coffee
300 ml/10 fl oz boiling water
1 sachet gelatine
3 tbsp cold water
1 tsp vanilla essence

1 tbsp coffee-flavoured liqueur (optional)
300 ml/10 fl oz double cream
4 chocolate-covered coffee beans
8 amaretti biscuits, to serve

1 Break the chocolate into small pieces and place in a saucepan with the coffee. Stir in the boiling water and heat gently, stirring, until the chocolate has melted.

2 Sprinkle the gelatine over the cold water and leave for 5 minutes, or until spongy, then whisk it into the chocolate to dissolve it.

3 Stir in the vanilla essence and coffee-flavoured liqueur, if using. Leave to stand in a cool place until just beginning to thicken, whisk occasionally.

4 Whip the cream until soft peaks form, then reserve a little for decorating the desserts and fold the remainder into the chocolate mixture. Spoon into 4 serving dishes and leave to set. Decorate with the reserved cream and coffee beans and serve with amaretti biscuits.

tiramisù

serves 8   **prep: 30 mins, plus 3 hrs chilling**   **cook: 30 mins**

Tiramisù is an Italian version of trifle. A wicked combination of mascarpone cheese, chocolate, coffee and rum makes this delicious dessert very rich and quite irresistible!

INGREDIENTS

butter, for greasing

3 eggs

140 g/5 oz golden caster sugar

90 g/3¼ oz self-raising flour

1 tbsp cocoa powder

150 ml/5 fl oz cold black coffee

2 tbsp rum

2 tsp cocoa powder, to decorate

FILLING

375 g/13 oz mascarpone cheese

225 ml/8 fl oz fresh custard

55 g/2 oz golden caster sugar

100 g/3½ oz plain chocolate, grated

variation

To save time, use sponge fingers instead of cake. Dip them in coffee and layer them with the mascarpone cheese mixture in a bowl.

cook's tip

Remove the mascarpone cheese from the refrigerator 30 minutes before using, to let it soften. This makes it easier to beat and to blend with the caster sugar.

1 Preheat the oven to 180°C/350°F/Gas Mark 4. To make the cake, grease a 20-cm/8-inch round cake tin with butter and line with baking paper. Place the eggs and sugar in a large bowl and beat together until thick and light. Sift the flour and cocoa powder over the mixture and fold in gently. Spoon the mixture into the prepared tin

and bake in the oven for 30 minutes, or until the cake springs back when pressed gently in the centre. Leave in the tin for 5 minutes, then turn out on to a wire rack to cool.

2 Place the black coffee and rum in a bowl or cup, mix together and reserve. To make the filling, place the mascarpone cheese in a

large bowl and beat until soft. Stir in the custard, then gradually add the sugar, beating constantly. Stir in the grated chocolate.

3 Cut the cake horizontally into 3 layers and place 1 layer on a serving plate. Sprinkle with one-third of the coffee mixture, then cover with

one-third of the mascarpone mixture. Repeat the layers, finishing with a topping of the mascarpone mixture. Leave to chill in the refrigerator for 3 hours. Sift over the cocoa powder before serving.

chocolate & amaretto cheesecake

cook: 1 hr 10 mins   **prep: 30 mins, plus 3 hrs chilling**   **serves 10–12**

Amaretto is an almond-flavoured Italian liqueur, which complements the plain chocolate and cream in this cheesecake perfectly.

variation

If you do not have any Amaretto liqueur, use another liqueur, such as Cointreau or brandy, instead.

cook's tip

To loosen the cheesecake, use a round-bladed knife to run around the inside, as a sharp knife may damage both the cake and the tin.

INGREDIENTS

oil, for brushing

175 g/6 oz digestive biscuits

55 g/2 oz amaretti biscuits

85 g/3 oz butter

3 tbsp plain flour

1 tsp vanilla essence

4 eggs

300 ml/10 fl oz double cream

50 ml/2 fl oz Amaretto liqueur

FILLING

225 g/8 oz plain chocolate

400 g/14 oz cream cheese, at room temperature

115 g/4 oz golden caster sugar

TOPPING

1 tbsp Amaretto liqueur

200 ml/7 fl oz crème fraîche

crushed amaretti biscuits

1 Line the base of a 23-cm/9-inch springform cake tin with foil and brush the sides with oil. Place the digestive and amaretti biscuits in a polythene bag and crush with a rolling pin. Place the butter in a saucepan and heat gently until just melted, then stir in the crushed biscuits. Press the mixture into the base of the tin and chill for 1 hour.

2 Preheat the oven to 160°C/325°F/Gas Mark 3. To make the filling, melt the chocolate (see pages 9–10) and leave to cool. Place the cream cheese in a bowl and beat until fluffy, then add the sugar, flour and vanilla essence and beat together until smooth. Gradually add the eggs, beating until well blended. Blend in the melted chocolate, cream and Amaretto liqueur. Pour the mixture over the chilled biscuit base and bake in the oven for 50–60 minutes, or until set.

3 Leave the cheesecake in the oven with the door slightly ajar, until cold. Run a knife around the inside of the tin to loosen the cheesecake. Leave to chill in the refrigerator for 2 hours, then remove from the tin and place on a serving plate. To make the topping, stir the Amaretto liqueur into the crème fraîche and spread over the cheesecake. Sprinkle the crushed amaretti biscuits around the edge to decorate.

marbled chocolate cheesecake

serves 10–12

prep: 45 mins, plus 3 hrs chilling

cook: 1 hr 10 mins

Cheesecake is always a favourite dessert, and this one, with marbled swirls of plain and white chocolate, is particularly appealing. It is perfect for an extra special occasion.

INGREDIENTS

oil, for brushing

225 g/8 oz plain chocolate digestive biscuits

85 g/3 oz butter

FILLING

700 g/1 lb 9 oz cream cheese

175 g/6 oz golden caster sugar

3 tbsp plain flour

2 tsp vanilla essence

3 eggs, beaten

115 g/4 oz plain chocolate, broken into pieces

115 g/4 oz white chocolate, broken into pieces

variation

A ginger-flavoured base would also work well – substitute ginger biscuits for the plain chocolate digestive biscuits.

cook's tip

Although it will take longer for the cheesecake to be ready, leaving it to cool in the oven with the door slightly ajar helps to prevent cracks appearing on the surface. Remove the cheesecake when it is completely cold.

1 Line the base of a 23-cm/9-inch springform tin with foil and brush the sides with oil. Place the biscuits in a polythene bag and crush with a rolling pin. Place the butter in a saucepan and heat gently until just melted, then stir in the crushed biscuits. Press into the base of the tin and chill in the refrigerator for 1 hour.

2 Preheat the oven to 160°C/325°F/Gas Mark 3. To make the filling, place the cream cheese in a bowl and beat until fluffy, then add the sugar, flour and vanilla essence and beat together until smooth. Gradually add the eggs, beating until well blended. Place half the mixture in a separate bowl. Melt the plain chocolate and white chocolate in 2 separate bowls (see pages 9–10) and leave to cool. Stir the plain chocolate into one bowl of cream cheese mixture and the white chocolate into the other.

3 Spoon the 2 mixtures alternately over the chilled biscuit base, then swirl with a knife to give a marbled effect. Bake in the preheated oven for 50–60 minutes, or until set. Leave the cheesecake in the oven with the door slightly ajar, until cold. Run a knife around the inside of the tin to loosen the cheesecake. Leave to chill in the refrigerator for 2 hours before removing from the tin to serve.

irish cream cheesecake

serves 12   **prep: 45 mins, plus 3 hrs chilling**   **cook: 10 mins**

This is an unbaked cheesecake, and although it is not set with gelatine, its high chocolate content ensures that it sets perfectly.

INGREDIENTS

oil, for brushing
175 g/6 oz chocolate chip cookies
55 g/2 oz butter

FILLING

225 g/8 oz plain chocolate
225 g/8 oz milk chocolate
55 g/2 oz golden caster sugar
350 g/12 oz cream cheese
425 ml/15 fl oz double cream, whipped
3 tbsp Irish cream liqueur

TO SERVE

crème fraîche
fresh fruit

cook's tip

Look out for miniature bottles of Irish cream liqueur, as they are a handy size for cooking. If you cannot find Irish cream liqueur, try using brandy.

1 Line the base of a 20-cm/8-inch springform tin with foil and brush the sides with oil. Place the cookies in a polythene bag and crush with a rolling pin. Place the butter in a saucepan and heat gently until just melted, then stir in the crushed biscuits. Press the mixture into the base of the tin and chill in the refrigerator for 1 hour.

2 To make the filling, melt the plain and milk chocolate together (see pages 9–10), stir to combine and leave to cool. Place the sugar and cream cheese in a large bowl and beat together until smooth, then fold in the whipped cream. Fold the mixture gently into the melted chocolate, then stir in the Irish cream liqueur.

3 Spoon the filling over the chilled biscuit base and smooth the surface. Cover and leave to chill in the refrigerator for 2 hours, or until quite firm. Transfer to a serving plate and cut into small slices. Serve with a spoonful of crème fraîche and fresh fruit.

chocolate wafer layers

cook: 5 mins

**prep: 50 mins, plus
30 mins–60 mins chilling**

serves 6

*Crisp delicate wafers of chocolate layered with a rich pistachio
cream filling taste as impressive as they look.*

cook's tip

Try not to overbeat the mascarpone
cheese filling, otherwise it will become
quite runny and difficult to spread over
the chocolate wafers.

INGREDIENTS

175 g/6 oz plain chocolate,
broken into pieces

250 g/9 oz mascarpone cheese

1 tbsp caster sugar

4 tbsp Tia Maria

300 ml/10 fl oz double cream

85 g/3 oz shelled, unsalted
pistachio nuts, chopped

115 g/4 oz milk chocolate, grated

1 Melt the chocolate (see
pages 9–10) and leave
to cool. Cut 6 strips of non-
stick baking paper measuring
6 x 27 cm/2½ x 10½ inches.
Brush evenly with the melted
chocolate. Mark each strip
with a knife every 9 cm/
3½ inches to make rectangles.
Leave in the refrigerator to set,
then carefully peel off the
chocolate wafers.

2 Place the mascarpone
cheese and sugar in a
bowl and beat together until
smooth. Beat in the Tia Maria
and cream until soft peaks
form. Fold in the pistachio nuts
and grated milk chocolate.

3 Arrange 6 chocolate
wafers on a tray
and spoon over half the
mascarpone cheese mixture.
Lay a second wafer on top of
each one and cover with the
remaining mixture. Top with a
final chocolate wafer. Leave to
chill in the refrigerator until
ready to serve.

chocolate brandy torte

cook: 10 mins　　　　**prep: 40 mins, plus 2 hrs chilling**　　　　**serves 12**

A crumbly ginger chocolate base topped with velvety smooth chocolate brandy cream makes this a blissful cake.

variation
If chocolate-covered coffee beans are unavailable, use chocolate-coated raisins to decorate instead.

cook's tip
When folding cream into the chocolate, do not overwork the mixture by mixing it too much as you want a light and fluffy end result.

INGREDIENTS

BASE

100 g/3½ oz butter, plus extra for greasing

250 g/9 oz gingernut biscuits

75 g/2¾ oz plain chocolate

300 ml/10 fl oz double cream

4 tbsp caster sugar

TO DECORATE

100 ml/3½ fl oz double cream

chocolate-covered coffee beans

FILLING

225 g/8 oz plain chocolate

250 g/9 oz mascarpone cheese

2 eggs, separated

3 tbsp brandy

1 Grease the base and sides of a 23-cm/9-inch springform cake tin. Place the biscuits in a polythene bag and crush with a rolling pin. Transfer to a bowl. Place the chocolate and butter in a small saucepan and heat gently until melted, then pour over the biscuits. Mix well, then press into the prepared tin. Leave to chill while preparing the filling.

2 To make the filling, place the chocolate in a heatproof bowl and set over a saucepan of simmering water, stirring, until melted. Remove from the heat and beat in the mascarpone cheese, egg yolks and brandy.

3 Whip the cream until just holding its shape. Fold in the chocolate mixture.

4 Whisk the egg whites in a spotlessly clean, greasefree bowl until soft peaks form. Add the sugar a little at a time and whisk until thick and glossy. Fold into the chocolate mixture, in 2 batches, until just mixed.

5 Spoon the mixture into the prepared base and leave to chill in the refrigerator for at least 2 hours. Carefully transfer to a serving plate. To decorate, whip the cream and pipe on to the cheesecake, add the chocolate-covered coffee beans and serve.

rich chocolate loaf

makes 16 slices
prep: 20 mins, plus 1 hr chilling
cook: 5 mins

Another rich chocolate dessert, this loaf is very simple to make and can be served as a teatime treat as well.

INGREDIENTS

75 g/2¾ oz almonds

150 g/5½ oz plain chocolate

6 tbsp unsalted butter

210 ml/7¼ fl oz condensed milk

2 tsp ground cinnamon

75 g/2¾ oz amaretti biscuits, broken

50 g/1¾ oz dried no-soak apricots, roughly chopped

cook's tip

To melt chocolate, first break it into manageable pieces. The smaller the pieces, the quicker it will melt. Remember to remove from the heat as soon as it has melted.

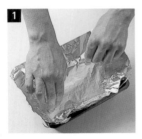

1 Line a 675-g/1lb 8-oz loaf tin with a piece of foil. Using a sharp knife, roughly chop the almonds and reserve until required.

2 Place the chocolate, butter, milk and cinnamon in a small heavy-based saucepan and heat over a low heat for 3–4 minutes, stirring constantly with a wooden spoon, or until the chocolate has melted. Remove from the heat and beat the mixture until well blended.

3 Stir the chopped almonds, biscuits and apricots into the chocolate mixture with a wooden spoon until thoroughly mixed.

4 Pour the mixture into the prepared tin and leave to chill in the refrigerator for 1 hour, or until set. Cut the loaf into slices to serve.

mississippi mud pie

⏱ **cook: 1 hr 10 mins**　　　🕐 **prep: 30 mins, plus 4 hrs cooling/chilling**　　　**serves 8**

An all-time favourite with chocoholics – the 'mud' refers to the gooey, rich chocolate layer of the cake.

cook's tip

To make sure the pastry cooks evenly and does not become too soggy, it is usually baked blind before the filling is added. Line with foil or baking paper and use baking beans or weights to hold it down.

INGREDIENTS

1 quantity of Basic Chocolate Pastry (see page 13)

plain flour, for dusting

175 g/6 oz butter

350 g/12 oz dark muscovado sugar

4 eggs, lightly beaten

4 tbsp cocoa powder, sifted

150 g/5½ oz plain chocolate

300 ml/10 fl oz single cream

1 tsp chocolate essence

TO DECORATE

425 ml/15 fl oz double cream, whipped

Chocolate Curls and Chocolate Flakes (see pages 10–12)

1 Preheat the oven to 190°C/375°F/Gas Mark 5. Make the pastry (see page 13) and leave to chill for 15 minutes. Roll out the dough on a lightly floured work surface and use to line a deep 23-cm/9-inch loose-bottomed flan tin. Line the case with foil and baking beans, then bake blind in the preheated oven for 15 minutes. Remove the beans,

and foil and cook for a further 10 minutes, or until the pastry case is crisp.

2 To make the filling, beat the butter and sugar together in a large bowl and gradually beat in the eggs with the cocoa powder. Melt the chocolate (see pages 9–10) and beat it into the mixture with the cream and chocolate essence.

3 Reduce the oven temperature to 160°C/325°F/Gas Mark 3. Pour the mixture into the cooked pastry case and bake in the oven for 45 minutes, or until the filling is set.

4 Leave the pie to cool completely, then transfer to a large serving plate. Cover with the whipped cream

and leave to chill in the refrigerator for 1 hour. Decorate the pie with Chocolate Curls and Chocolate Flakes and leave to chill in the refrigerator for 2 hours before serving.

chocolate chiffon pie

serves 8 **prep: 35 mins, plus 4 hrs** ⟲
30 mins cooling/chilling

cook: 12–15 mins ⟳

*The nutty crust of this delectable American pie contrasts with the
tempting creamy chocolate filling. Serve with cream, if you like.*

INGREDIENTS

2 tbsp chopped Brazil nuts, plus extra
to decorate

2 tbsp granulated sugar

2 tsp melted butter

225 ml/8 fl oz milk

2 tsp gelatine

115 g/4 oz caster sugar

2 eggs, separated

225 g/8 oz plain chocolate,
roughly chopped

1 tsp vanilla essence

150 ml/5 fl oz double cream

variation

If you like, replace the nut base with
either a Chocolate Biscuit Base
(see page 58) or a Rich Chocolate
Pastry Base (see page 13).

cook's tip

When dissolving gelatine in a bowl set
over a saucepan of simmering water,
do not let the gelatine mixture boil or
overheat, otherwise the gelatine will
become stringy and may spoil the
finished dessert.

1 Preheat the oven to
200°C/400°F/Gas
Mark 6. Place the nuts in a
food processor and process
until finely ground. Add the
granulated sugar and butter
and process briefly. Transfer
the mixture to a 23-cm/9-inch
round springform tin and press
it on to the base and sides
with a spoon. Bake for 8–10
minutes, or until golden. Cool.

2 Pour the milk into the
top of a double boiler or
into a heatproof bowl and
sprinkle the gelatine on the top.
Leave to soften for 2 minutes,
then place over a saucepan of
simmering water. Stir in half the
caster sugar, both the egg yolks
and all the chocolate. Stir over a
low heat for 4–5 minutes, or
until the gelatine has dissolved
and the chocolate has melted.

Remove from the heat and beat
until smooth and blended. Stir
in the vanilla essence, cover and
chill in the refrigerator for
45–60 minutes, or until just
beginning to set.

3 Whip the cream until
stiff, then fold all but
3 tablespoons into the
chocolate mixture. Whisk the
egg whites in a spotlessly clean

bowl until soft peaks form. Add
2 teaspoons of the remaining
caster sugar and whisk until
stiff peaks form. Fold in the
remaining sugar, then fold the
egg whites on to the chocolate
mixture. Pour the filling on to
the base and chill for 3 hours,
or until set. Decorate the pie
with the remaining whipped
cream and the chopped nuts
before serving.

chocolate trifle

cook: 10 mins   **prep: 45 mins, plus 2 hrs 30 mins cooling/chilling**   **serves 8**

This is a wonderful dessert for a party. It makes a change from a conventional trifle, and is served with chocolate truffles and fruit.

variation

If you like, replace the raspberry jam with blackcurrant jam and use mixed berries, such as blackcurrants and raspberries, to decorate.

cook's tip

Frozen packets of fruit are available in most supermarkets. Sometimes they are described as 'summer fruits' or 'fruits of the forest'. Try to find a variety that includes cherries.

INGREDIENTS

280 g/10 oz ready-made chocolate loaf cake

3–4 tbsp seedless raspberry jam

4 tbsp Amaretto liqueur

250 g/9 oz packet frozen mixed red fruit, thawed

CUSTARD

6 egg yolks

55 g/2 oz golden caster sugar

1 tbsp cornflour

500 ml/18 fl oz milk

55 g/2 oz plain chocolate, melted (see pages 9–10)

TOPPING

225 ml/8 fl oz double cream

1 tbsp golden caster sugar

½ tsp vanilla essence

TO DECORATE

ready-made chocolate truffles

fresh fruit, such as cherries and strawberries

1 Cut the cake into slices and make 'sandwiches' with the raspberry jam. Cut the sandwiches into cubes and place in a large serving bowl. Sprinkle with the Amaretto liqueur. Spoon the fruit over the cake.

2 To make the custard, place the egg yolks and sugar in a heatproof bowl and whisk until thick and pale, then stir in the cornflour. Place the milk in a saucepan and heat until almost boiling. Pour on to the egg yolk mixture, stirring. Return the mixture to the saucepan and bring just to the boil, stirring constantly, until it thickens. Remove from the heat and leave to cool slightly. Stir in the melted chocolate. Pour the custard over the cake and fruit. Cool, then cover and leave to chill in the refrigerator for 2 hours, or until set.

3 To make the topping, whip the cream until soft peaks form, then beat in the sugar and vanilla essence. Spoon over the trifle. Decorate with truffles and fruit and chill until ready to serve.

hot desserts

Because so few people these days either eat or cook puddings or baked desserts on a regular basis, they tend to be regarded as something of a treat. Nothing is guaranteed to please your family and friends more than the sight of a hot chocolate pudding at the end of a meal! Despite the fact that many of these hot desserts are actually easier to prepare than elaborate chilled desserts, your guests will feel extra pampered and indulged when they are served these home-made delights.

Some of the following recipes are based on tried-and-trusted favourites, but with an added dimension, such as Chocolate Bread & Butter Pudding (see page 86) and Steamed Chocolate Pudding (see page 96), while dishes like Chocolate Fondue (see page 76), Baked Peaches with Chocolate (see page 73) and Barbecued Chocolate Bananas (see page 80) are deceptively simple to make. Others, such as Exotic Fruit Chocolate Crêpes (see page 74) and Chocolate Cake with Rosemary Custard (see page 92) are full of exotic and fragrant flavours. Many of the desserts can be made in advance and reheated just before serving, and none requires elaborate decoration or presentation. So give your guests something really special, and sit back and enjoy the compliments!

ginger pears with chocolate sauce

serves 4   **prep: 20 mins** ⟲   **cook: 20–25 mins** ⏱

Pears and chocolate form another highly successful partnership in this simple dessert that is extremely easy to make.

INGREDIENTS

4 dessert pears
450 ml/16 fl oz water
150 g/5½ oz golden caster sugar
10-cm/4-inch piece fresh root ginger,
peeled and sliced
½ cinnamon stick
dash of lemon juice

SAUCE
4 tbsp single cream
200 g/7 oz plain chocolate,
broken into pieces

cook's tip

Choose unblemished dessert pears that are ripe but still firm, so that they keep their shape when cooked. Suitable varieties include Comice and Packham pears.

1 Peel the pears, leaving the stalks intact. Cut the base of each pear so that it sits upright. Carefully remove as much of the core as possible with a small spoon.

2 Place the water, sugar, ginger, cinnamon stick and lemon juice in a small, heavy-based saucepan. Bring to the boil and boil for 5 minutes. Stand the pears upright in the saucepan and cook, turning occasionally, for 15–20 minutes, or until softened. Place each pear on a serving plate.

3 To make the chocolate sauce, place the cream and chocolate in a heatproof bowl and set over a saucepan of gently simmering water until the chocolate has melted. Stir until smooth. Transfer to a jug and serve immediately with the warm pears.

baked peaches with chocolate

cook: 30 mins   **prep: 15 mins**   **serves 4**

This is a delicious variation on the classic Italian pairing of peaches baked with a filling of amaretti biscuits.

cook's tip

Choose peaches that are ripe but firm. If they are overripe, they will collapse during cooking. Use a sharp knife to cut the peeled peaches, then carefully prise out and discard the stone, leaving the peach half intact.

INGREDIENTS

25 g/1 oz unsalted butter, softened, plus extra for greasing

85 g/3 oz amaretti biscuits, roughly crushed

25 g/1 oz plain chocolate, finely grated

4 large peaches

1 tbsp golden caster sugar

crème fraîche, to serve

1 Preheat the oven to 190°C/375°F/Gas Mark 5. Grease a shallow baking dish with butter. Place the biscuits, grated chocolate and butter in a bowl and mix together. Place the peaches in a separate heatproof bowl and cover with boiling water. Leave for 1 minute, then transfer to a bowl of cold water and leave for a further 1 minute.

2 Remove the peaches from the water and peel off the skins. Cut each peach in half and remove the stone. Using a teaspoon, scoop out a little flesh from each peach half. Chop the flesh and add to the biscuit mixture.

3 Fill each peach half with the amaretti biscuit mixture, then sprinkle with sugar. Bake in the preheated oven for 30 minutes, or until the peaches are soft and the filling is crisp. Transfer to a large serving plate and serve hot with crème fraîche.

exotic fruit chocolate crêpes

serves 4

prep: 15 mins, plus 20 mins standing

cook: 15 mins

Everybody loves crêpes, and when they are filled with exotic fruit, they are impossible to resist. Dust with icing sugar and eat at once.

INGREDIENTS

100 g/3½ oz plain flour
2 tbsp cocoa powder
pinch of salt
1 egg, beaten
300 ml/10 fl oz milk
oil, for frying
icing sugar, for dusting

FILLING

100 g/3½ oz Greek-style natural yogurt
250 g/9 oz mascarpone cheese
icing sugar (optional)
1 mango, peeled and diced
225 g/8 oz strawberries, hulled and quartered
2 passion fruit

variation

Other combinations of fruit would also work well, such as mixed summer berries or raspberries, bananas, pears and apples.

cook's tip

The crêpes can be made in advance, then wrapped in foil and reheated in a warm oven. Make sure the crêpes are thoroughly heated through before filling and serving.

1 To make the filling, place the yogurt and mascarpone cheese in a bowl and sweeten with icing sugar, if you like. Place the mango and strawberries in a bowl and mix together. Cut the passion fruit in half, scoop out the pulp and seeds and add to the mango and strawberries. Stir together, then reserve.

2 To make the crêpes, sift the flour, cocoa powder and salt into a bowl and make a well in the centre. Add the egg and whisk well with a balloon whisk. Gradually beat in the milk, drawing in the flour from the sides, to make a smooth batter. Cover and leave to stand for 20 minutes. Heat a small amount of oil in an 18-cm/7-inch crêpe pan or

frying pan. Pour in just enough batter to thinly coat the base of the pan. Cook over a medium–high heat for 1 minute, then turn and cook the other side for 30–60 seconds, or until cooked through.

3 Transfer the crêpe to a plate and keep hot. Repeat with the remaining

batter, stacking the cooked crêpes on top of each other with greaseproof paper in between. Keep warm in the oven while cooking the remainder. Divide the filling between the crêpes, then roll up and dust with icing sugar. Serve immediately.

chocolate fondue

cook: 5 mins   **prep: 20 mins**   **serves 6**

*Chilled fresh fruit dipped into a warm chocolate sauce makes a
simple yet sumptuous dessert. It is perfect for entertaining guests.*

variation

If serving to children, substitute orange
juice for the brandy. In addition to fruit
for dipping, serve pieces of cake,
biscuits, meringues or marshmallows.

cook's tip

If you do not have a fondue pot,
simply melt the chocolate in a small
saucepan and transfer to an attractive
bowl for serving. The chocolate will
thicken more quickly than if it is kept
warm over a burner.

INGREDIENTS

1 pineapple

1 mango

12 Cape gooseberries

250 g/9 oz fresh strawberries

250 g/9 oz seedless green grapes

FONDUE

250 g/9 oz plain chocolate,

broken into pieces

150 ml/5 fl oz double cream

2 tbsp brandy

1 Using a sharp knife,
peel and core the
pineapple, then cut the flesh
into cubes. Peel the mango
and cut the flesh into cubes.
Peel back the papery outer
skin of the Cape gooseberries
and twist at the top to make a
'handle'. Arrange all the fruit
on 6 serving plates and leave
to chill in the refrigerator.

2 To make the fondue,
place the chocolate and
cream in a fondue pot. Heat
gently, stirring constantly, until
the chocolate has melted. Stir
in the brandy until thoroughly
blended and the chocolate
mixture is smooth.

3 Place the fondue pot
over the burner to keep
warm. To serve, allow each
guest to dip the fruit into the
sauce, using fondue forks or
bamboo skewers.

chocolate fruit crumble

serves 4   **prep: 10 mins** ⏲   **cook: 40–45 mins** ⏲

The addition of chocolate in a crumble topping makes it even more of a treat, and it is also a good way of enticing children to eat a fruit dessert.

INGREDIENTS

6 tbsp butter, plus extra for greasing

400 g/14 oz canned apricots, in natural juice

450 g/1 lb cooking apples, peeled and thickly sliced

100 g/3½ oz plain flour

50 g/1¾ oz porridge oats

4 tbsp caster sugar

100 g/3½ oz chocolate chips

variation

Other fruits can be used – pears with fresh or frozen raspberries work well. If you do not use canned fruit, add 4 tablespoons of orange juice to the fruit.

1 Preheat the oven to 350°F/180°C/Gas Mark 4. Grease an ovenproof dish with a little butter.

2 Drain the apricots, reserving 4 tablespoons of the juice. Place the apples and apricots in the prepared ovenproof dish with the reserved apricot juice and toss to mix thoroughly.

3 Sift the flour into a large bowl. Cut the butter into small cubes and rub it in with your fingertips until the mixture resembles fine breadcrumbs. Stir in the porridge oats, caster sugar and chocolate chips.

4 Sprinkle the crumble mixture over the apples and apricots and smooth the top roughly. Do not press the crumble down on to the fruit. Bake in the preheated oven for 40–45 minutes, or until the topping is golden. Serve the crumble hot or cold.

chocolate eve's pudding

cook: 50 mins   **prep: 15 mins**   **serves 4**

Eve's Pudding is traditionally made with apples, but here it is made with fresh raspberries and white chocolate sponge, with a tasty bitter chocolate sauce.

variation

Try using plain chocolate instead of white chocolate, and top with apricot halves, covered with peach schnapps and apricot conserve.

INGREDIENTS

2 eating apples

225 g/8 oz fresh or frozen raspberries

4 tbsp seedless raspberry jam

2 tbsp port (optional)

TOPPING

4 tbsp soft margarine

4 tbsp caster sugar

75 g/2¾ oz self-raising flour, sifted

50 g/1¾ oz white chocolate, grated

1 egg

2 tbsp milk

Chocolate Sauce (see page 13)

1 Preheat the oven to 180°C/350°F/Gas Mark 4. Peel, core and slice the apples. Place in a shallow 1.2-litre/2-pint ovenproof dish with the raspberries.

2 Place the raspberry jam and port, if using, in a small saucepan and heat gently until the jam melts and blends with the port. Pour the mixture over the fruit.

3 Place the margarine, sugar, flour, white chocolate, egg and milk in a bowl and mix until smooth. Spoon the mixture over the fruit and smooth the top.

4 Bake in the hot oven for 40–45 minutes, or until the top is springy to the touch. Make the Chocolate Sauce, then serve warm with the pudding.

barbecued chocolate bananas

serves 4   **prep: 5 mins** ⏱   **cook: 10 mins** ⏱

This is a simple dessert to serve at the end of a barbecue. Open up the foil parcels carefully as they are hot. Serve with whipped cream.

INGREDIENTS

4 bananas

50 g/1¾ oz chocolate drops

50 g/1¾ oz mini marshmallows

whipped cream, to serve

variation
For a fruitier flavour, add a selection of other fruits to each parcel, such as whole strawberries and raspberries, or peach and mango slices.

1 Using a sharp knife, slit the banana skins and almost through the bananas. Push chocolate drops and marshmallows into the slits, then wrap tightly in foil.

2 Place the banana and chocolate parcels on a grill rack and cook over hot coals on a preheated barbecue for 10 minutes, turning after 5 minutes.

3 Open up the parcels carefully and serve the bananas with whipped cream.

cherry & chocolate clafoutis

cook: 50–60 mins   **prep: 15 mins**   **serves 6–8**

Clafoutis is a traditional dessert from the South of France made with black cherries, and chocolate and kirsch makes it taste superb.

variation

Other fruit, such as plums or apples, can be used instead of the black cherries, if they are unavailable.

cook's tip

The clafoutis can be served straight from the oven, but it is best if it is left to cool slightly, then served warm with a little cream.

INGREDIENTS

butter, for greasing
450 g/1 lb black cherries, stoned
25 g/1 oz golden granulated sugar
3 eggs
55 g/2 oz golden caster sugar
55 g/2 oz self-raising flour
15 g/½ oz cocoa powder
150 ml/5 fl oz double cream
300 ml/10 fl oz milk
2 tbsp kirsch (optional)
cream, to serve

TO DECORATE
icing sugar
fresh whole black cherries

1 Preheat the oven to 190°C/375°F/Gas Mark 5. Lightly grease a 23-cm/9-inch ovenproof flan or tart dish with butter. Arrange the cherries in the dish, sprinkle with the granulated sugar and reserve.

2 Place the eggs and caster sugar in a bowl and whisk together until light and frothy. Sift the flour and cocoa powder on to a plate and add, all at once, to the egg mixture. Beat in thoroughly, then whisk in the cream, followed by the milk and kirsch, if using. Pour the batter over the cherries.

3 Bake in the preheated oven for 50–60 minutes, or until slightly risen and set in the centre. Sift icing sugar over and decorate with a few fresh cherries. Serve warm with cream.

chocolate apple pie

cook: 40 mins

prep: 25 mins, plus 30 mins chilling

serves 6

Easy-to-make crumbly chocolate pastry encases a delicious apple filling studded with chocolate chips – a guaranteed family favourite.

cook's tip

When making pastry, use as little cold water as possible to bind the dough because adding too much makes the dough sticky and difficult to handle.

INGREDIENTS

4 tbsp cocoa powder

200 g/7 oz plain flour, plus extra for dusting

100 g/3½ oz softened butter

4 tbsp caster sugar

2 egg yolks

few drops of vanilla essence

1–2 tbsp cold water

FILLING

750 g/1 lb 10 oz cooking apples

2 tbsp butter

½ tsp ground cinnamon

50 g/1¾ oz plain chocolate chips

egg white, beaten

½ tsp caster sugar, for sprinkling

1 To make the pastry, sieve the cocoa powder and flour into a large bowl, add the butter and rub it in until the mixture resembles fine breadcrumbs. Stir in the sugar. Add the egg yolks, vanilla essence and enough water to mix to a dough.

2 Roll out the dough on a lightly floured surface and use to line a deep 20-cm/8-inch flan or cake tin. Leave to chill in the refrigerator for 30 minutes. Roll out any trimmings and cut out some pastry leaves to decorate the top of the pie.

3 Preheat the oven to 180°C/350°F/Gas Mark 4. Peel, core and thickly slice the apples. Place half the apple slices in a heavy-based saucepan with the butter and cinnamon and cook over a low heat, stirring occasionally, until the apples soften.

4 Stir in the uncooked apple slices, leave to cool slightly, then stir in the chocolate chips. Prick the base of the pastry case and pile the apple mixture into it. Arrange the pastry leaves on top. Brush the leaves with a little egg white and sprinkle with caster sugar.

5 Bake in the preheated oven for 35 minutes, or until the pastry is crisp. Serve warm or cold.

pecan & chocolate pie

⏲ **cook: 40–45 mins**   ⏱ **prep: 25 mins**   **serves 6–8**

Pecan pie is an all-time American favourite. Adding
chocolate makes it even more luxurious.

variation

If you like, replace the Rich Shortcrust Pastry with the Basic Chocolate Pastry (see page 13) and serve with crème fraîche instead of whipped cream.

cook's tip

When rolling out pastry, do not use too much flour, as this changes the texture of the pastry, and remember to roll in one direction only. Cover the pie with foil if the pastry becomes too brown while baking.

INGREDIENTS

1 quantity Rich Shortcrust
Pastry (see page 13)
whipped cream, to serve
ground cinnamon, for dusting

FILLING
55 g/2 oz butter
3 tbsp cocoa powder
225 ml/8 fl oz golden syrup
3 eggs
70 g/2½ oz dark muscovado sugar
175 g/6 oz shelled pecan nuts, chopped

1 Roll out the chilled dough on a lightly floured work surface and use to line a 20-cm/8-inch flan tin.

2 Preheat the oven to 190°C/375°F/Gas Mark 5. To make the filling, place the butter in a small, heavy-based saucepan and heat gently until melted. Sift in the cocoa and stir in the syrup.

3 Place the eggs and sugar in a large bowl and beat together. Add the syrup mixture and the chopped pecan nuts and stir. Pour the mixture into the prepared pastry case.

4 Place the pie on a preheated baking sheet and bake in the preheated oven for 35–40 minutes, or until the filling is just set. Leave to cool slightly and serve warm with a spoonful of whipped cream, dusted with ground cinnamon.

chocolate bread & butter pudding

serves 6   **prep: 15 mins, plus** 🕒
10 mins soaking   **cook: 1 hr** 🕒

*This traditional nursery pudding is given a brand new twist
with plain chocolate added to the custard.*

INGREDIENTS

70 g/2½ oz butter, softened, plus
extra for greasing

600 ml/1 pint milk

150 ml/5 fl oz double cream

75 g/2¾ oz plain chocolate,
broken into pieces

6 thick slices of fruit bread

3 eggs

55 g/2 oz golden caster sugar

1 tbsp demerara sugar

1 tsp ground cinnamon

variation

Instead of using fruit bread, use white
bread and sprinkle some dried fruit in
between the slices.

cook's tip

This pudding is cooked in a bain-marie,
which is a roasting tin filled with
water. This helps to slow down the
cooking process and prevent the egg
custard curdling.

1 Preheat the oven
to 180°C/350°F/Gas
Mark 4. Grease a 1.4-litre/
2½-pint shallow ovenproof
dish with butter. Place the
milk, cream and chocolate in
a heavy-based saucepan and
heat gently until the chocolate
has melted. Butter the slices
of bread and cut into triangles.
Arrange the bread in the
prepared dish.

2 Whisk the eggs and
caster sugar into the
chocolate milk and pour over
the bread. Leave to soak for
10 minutes. Gently push the
bread down into the custard.

3 Place the demerara
sugar and cinnamon in
a small bowl and mix together.
Sprinkle over the top of the
pudding. Place the dish in a
roasting tin and pour in
enough hot water to come
halfway up the sides of the
dish. Bake in the preheated
oven for 50–55 minutes, or
until the custard is lightly set
and the top is golden brown.

chocolate queen of puddings

⏲ **cook: 40–45 mins**   ⏱ **prep: 25 mins**   **serves 4**

An old time favourite with an up-to-date twist, this pudding makes the perfect end to a special family meal.

variation

If you like, add 40 g/1½ oz desiccated coconut to the breadcrumbs and omit the black cherry jam.

cook's tip

To achieve the best results when making meringue, make sure that all your utensils and bowls are very clean and free from any grease, otherwise the egg whites will not whisk up successfully.

INGREDIENTS

50 g/1¾ oz plain chocolate

450 ml/16 fl oz chocolate-flavoured milk

100 g/3½ oz fresh white or

wholemeal breadcrumbs

125 g/4½ oz caster sugar

2 eggs, separated

4 tbsp black cherry jam

1 Preheat the oven to 180°C/350°F/Gas Mark 4. Break the chocolate into small pieces and place in a small, heavy-based saucepan with the chocolate-flavoured milk. Heat gently, stirring constantly, until the chocolate melts. Bring almost to the boil, then remove the saucepan from the heat.

2 Place the breadcrumbs in a large bowl with 25 g/1 oz of the sugar. Pour over the chocolate milk and mix well. Beat in the egg yolks.

3 Spoon the mixture into a 1.2-litre/2-pint pie dish and bake in the preheated oven for 25–30 minutes, or until set and firm to the touch.

4 Whisk the egg whites in a large, spotlessly clean, greasefree bowl until soft peaks form. Gradually whisk in the remaining sugar and whisk until you have a thick, glossy meringue.

5 Spread the black cherry jam over the surface of the chocolate mixture and pile or pipe the meringue on top. Return to the oven for 15 minutes, or until the meringue is crisp and golden. Serve immediately.

chocolate meringue pie

serves 6 **prep: 25 mins** ⏱ **cook: 35 mins** ⏱

Crumbly biscuit base, rich creamy chocolate filling topped with fluffy meringue – what could be more indulgent than this dessert?

INGREDIENTS

225 g/8 oz plain chocolate
digestive biscuits

4 tbsp butter

FILLING

3 egg yolks

4 tbsp caster sugar

4 tbsp cornflour

600 ml/1 pint milk

100 g/3½ oz plain chocolate, melted
(see pages 9–10)

MERINGUE

2 egg whites

100 g/3½ oz caster sugar

¼ tsp vanilla essence

variation

Instead of the plain chocolate biscuits, you can use either ginger biscuits or even amaretti biscuits.

cook's tip

When cooking with chocolate, try to find the chocolate with the highest cocoa butter content as this gives a far superior taste.

1 Preheat the oven to 160°C/375°F/Gas Mark 3. Place the biscuits in a polythene bag and crush with a rolling pin, then transfer to a large bowl. Place the butter in a saucepan and heat gently until just melted, then stir it into the biscuit crumbs until well mixed. Press into the base and up the sides of a 23-cm/9-inch flan tin or dish.

2 To make the filling, place the egg yolks, caster sugar and cornflour in a large bowl and beat until they form a smooth paste, adding a little of the milk, if necessary. Place the milk into a small, heavy-based saucepan and heat gently until almost boiling, then slowly pour it on to the egg mixture, whisking well.

3 Return the mixture to the saucepan and cook gently, whisking, until thick. Remove from the heat. Whisk in the melted chocolate, then pour it on to the biscuit base.

4 To make the meringue, whisk the egg whites in a large, spotlessly clean, greasefree bowl until soft peaks form. Gradually whisk in two-thirds of the sugar until the mixture is stiff and glossy. Fold in the remaining sugar and vanilla essence.

5 Spread the meringue over the filling, swirling the surface with the back of a spoon to give it an attractive finish. Bake in the centre of the oven for 30 minutes, or until golden. Serve hot or just warm.

chocolate cake with rosemary custard

serves 8   **prep: 25 mins, plus** ⏲   **cook: 1 hr 20 mins** ⏲
40 mins cooling/infusing

This cake is good served cold, but it is even more special when served warm with a delicate rosemary-flavoured custard.

INGREDIENTS

115 g/4 oz unsalted butter, plus extra for greasing

150 g/5½ oz plain chocolate, broken into pieces

3 large eggs, separated, plus 1 extra egg white

115 g/4 oz golden caster sugar

¾ tsp cream of tartar

2 tbsp plain flour

1 tsp ground cinnamon

20 g/¾ oz ground almonds

icing sugar, for dusting

fresh rosemary sprigs, to decorate

CUSTARD

2 fresh rosemary sprigs

1 vanilla pod, split

300 ml/10 fl oz single cream

150 ml/5 fl oz milk

5 large egg yolks

40 g/1½ oz golden caster sugar

---

variation

As an alternative to rosemary, the custard could be flavoured with orange rind, bay leaves, brandy or a liqueur of your choice.

---

cook's tip

Use a sharp knife to split the vanilla pod in half lengthways and use a slotted spoon to remove the pod from the custard before serving.

1 Preheat the oven to 180°C/350°F/Gas Mark 4. Grease and line the base of a 22-cm/8½-inch round cake tin. Place the chocolate and butter in a heatproof bowl and set over a saucepan of simmering water until melted. Stir in the egg yolks and half the sugar. Place the egg whites and cream of tartar in a clean bowl and beat until soft peaks form. Gradually beat in the remaining sugar until stiff but not dry. Sift the flour and cinnamon into another bowl and stir in the almonds. Fold into the egg white mixture, then fold this mixture into the chocolate mixture.

2 Spoon into the cake tin and stand in a roasting tin. Pour in enough hot water to come halfway up the sides of the tin. Bake for 1 hour– 1 hour 10 minutes, or until firm to the touch. Remove from the roasting tin, cover and leave for 10 minutes before turning out and placing on a wire rack to cool slightly.

3 Make the custard. Heat the rosemary, vanilla pod, cream and milk in a pan until almost boiling. Remove from the heat and leave to infuse for 30 minutes. Beat the egg yolks and sugar together until thick and pale. Reheat the cream mixture, sieve on to the egg mixture and whisk in. Set the bowl over a pan of simmering water and stir until thick. Dust the cake with icing sugar, decorate with rosemary and serve with the custard.

chocolate cranberry sponge

cook: 1 hr 10 mins   **prep: 20 mins**   **serves 4**

*The sharpness of the fruit contrasts deliciously with the sweetness
of the chocolate in this wonderful, fluffy sponge pudding.*

variation

Serve with Chocolate Sauce (see
page 13) and add 1 tablespoon
of brandy or rum to the chocolate
and cream.

cook's tip

If you don't have a steamer, place
the basin on a foil sling in a large
saucepan and fill with enough water
to come halfway up the sides of the
basin. Cook as in main recipe, then
use the sling to remove the basin.

INGREDIENTS

4 tbsp unsalted butter, plus
extra for greasing
4 tbsp dark brown sugar, plus
extra for sprinkling
85 g/3 oz cranberries, thawed if frozen
1 large cooking apple
2 eggs, lightly beaten
85 g/3 oz self-raising flour
3 tbsp cocoa powder

SAUCE
175 g/6 oz plain chocolate
400 ml/14 fl oz evaporated milk
1 tsp vanilla essence
½ tsp almond essence

1 Grease a 1.2-litre/2-pint
pudding basin with a
little butter, then sprinkle with
brown sugar to coat the sides.
Tip out any excess. Place the
cranberries in a large bowl.
Using a sharp knife, peel,
core and dice the apple and
mix with the cranberries, then
place the fruit in the prepared
pudding basin.

2 Place the butter, sugar
and eggs in a large
bowl. Sift in the flour and
cocoa powder and beat until
well mixed. Pour the mixture
on top of the fruit, then cover
with foil and tie with string.
Place the bowl in a steamer set
over a saucepan of simmering
water and steam for 1 hour, or
until risen, topping up with
boiling water, as necessary.

3 Meanwhile, make the
sauce. Break the
chocolate into pieces and place
in a heatproof bowl set over a
saucepan of simmering water
with the milk. Stir constantly,
until the chocolate has melted,
then remove the bowl from
the heat. Whisk in the vanilla
and almond essences and beat
until thick and smooth.

4 To serve, remove the
pudding and discard the
foil. Run a round-bladed knife
around the side of the basin,
place a serving plate on top of
the pudding and, holding them
together, invert. Serve
immediately with the sauce.

steamed chocolate pudding

This is as far removed from a school dinner steamed pudding as anything could possibly be! It is best served as soon as it is cooked.

INGREDIENTS

115 g/4 oz butter, softened,
plus extra for greasing
115 g/4 oz light muscovado sugar
2 eggs, beaten
85 g/3 oz self-raising flour
25 g/1 oz cocoa powder
1–2 tbsp milk (optional)
100 g/3½ oz plain chocolate chips

SAUCE

55 g/2 oz butter
55 g/2 oz light muscovado sugar
3 tbsp brandy
55 g/2 oz blanched whole hazelnuts
55 g/2 oz luxury mixed dried fruit

cook's tip

You can make the pudding in advance. Place the covered basin back into a saucepan of boiling water, on a trivet, for 20–30 minutes before serving.

1 Grease a 1.2-litre/2-pint pudding basin and line the base with a small round of greaseproof paper. Beat the butter and sugar together until light and fluffy. Gradually beat in the eggs. Sift the flour and cocoa powder into the mixture and fold in. Add a little milk, if necessary, to make a dropping consistency. Stir in the chocolate chips.

2 Spoon the mixture into the prepared basin. Cut out a round of greaseproof paper and a round of foil, both about 7.5 cm/3 inches larger than the top of the basin. Place the paper on top of the foil and grease the upper surface. Make a fold in the centre of both, then use to cover the basin, paper-side down, and secure with string.

Place the basin on a trivet in a saucepan and pour in enough boiling water to come halfway up the sides of the basin. Cover and simmer for 1½ hours, topping up with boiling water as necessary.

3 To make the sauce, place the butter and sugar in a small saucepan and heat gently until the sugar has

dissolved and the mixture looks slightly caramelized. Add the brandy and leave to bubble for 1 minute. Stir in the hazelnuts and dried fruit. Carefully turn the pudding out on to a plate and spoon the sauce over. Serve immediately.

individual chocolate fondant puddings

 cook: 20 mins   prep: 15 mins   serves 4

As you cut into these tasty puddings, you will discover their seductive warm liquid chocolate centres.

variation

For a truly tempting presentation, you can also serve these puddings with a raspberry coulis and a few fresh raspberries on the side.

INGREDIENTS

100 g/3½ oz butter,
plus extra for greasing
100 g/3½ oz golden caster sugar,
plus extra for coating
100 g/3½ oz plain chocolate,
broken into pieces
2 large eggs
1 tsp vanilla essence
2 tbsp plain flour
icing sugar, for dusting
vanilla ice cream, to serve

1 Preheat the oven to 200°C/400°F/Gas Mark 6. Grease 4 x 175-ml/6-fl oz pudding basins or ramekin dishes and coat with caster sugar. Place the butter and chocolate in a heatproof bowl and set over a saucepan of gently simmering water until melted. Stir until smooth. Leave to cool.

2 Place the eggs, vanilla essence, caster sugar and flour in a bowl and whisk together. Stir in the melted chocolate. Pour the mixture into the prepared moulds and place on a baking tray. Bake in the oven for 12–15 minutes, or until the puddings are well risen and set on the outside but still melting inside.

3 Leave to stand for 1 minute, then turn the puddings out on to 4 serving plates. Dust with icing sugar and serve immediately with vanilla ice cream.

saucy chocolate pudding

serves 4–6   **prep: 10 mins** ⟲   **cook: 50–60 mins** ⟲

When you first remove this pudding from the oven, it doesn't look particularly impressive. However, when you cut into it, you find a lovely pool of chocolate sauce at the bottom of the dish.

INGREDIENTS

85 g/3 oz butter, softened,
plus extra for greasing
55 g/2 oz self-raising flour
25 g/1 oz cocoa powder
1 tsp ground cinnamon
115 g/4 oz golden caster sugar
1 egg
25 g/1 oz dark muscovado sugar
55 g/2 oz shelled pecan nuts, chopped
300 ml/10 fl oz hot black coffee
icing sugar, for dusting
whipped cream, to serve

cook's tip

Take care not to open the oven for the first 40 minutes of the cooking time, otherwise the pudding may sink quite considerably.

1 Preheat the oven to 160°C/325°F/Gas Mark 3. Grease a shallow 1.2-litre/2-pint ovenproof dish with a little butter. Sift the flour, cocoa powder and cinnamon into a large bowl. Add the butter, 85 g/3 oz of the caster sugar and the egg and beat together until the

mixture is well blended. Turn into the prepared dish and sprinkle with the muscovado sugar and the pecan nuts.

2 Pour the coffee into a large jug, stir in the remaining caster sugar until dissolved and carefully pour over the pudding.

3 Bake in the hot oven for 50–60 minutes, or until firm to the touch in the centre. Dust with a little icing sugar and serve immediately with whipped cream.

cappuccino soufflé puddings

 cook: 20 mins   **prep: 25 mins**   **serves 6**

These light and airy puddings simply melt in the mouth. Served with vanilla ice cream, they will provide the perfect finale to any meal.

variation

Kahlua is a liqueur with a distinctive coffee flavour, but if you cannot find it, substitute rum or brandy as an alternative flavouring.

INGREDIENTS

butter, for greasing

25 g/1 oz golden caster sugar, plus extra for coating

6 tbsp whipping cream

2 tsp instant espresso coffee granules

2 tbsp Kahlua

3 large eggs, separated, plus 1 extra egg white

150 g/5½ oz plain chocolate, melted and cooled (see pages 9–10)

cocoa powder, for dusting

vanilla ice cream, to serve

1 Preheat the oven to 190°C/375°F/Gas Mark 5. Grease the sides of 6 x 175-ml/6-fl oz ramekin dishes with butter and coat with caster sugar. Place on a baking tray.

2 Place the cream in a small, heavy-based saucepan and heat gently. Stir in the coffee until it has dissolved, then stir in the Kahlua. Divide the coffee mixture between the prepared ramekin dishes.

3 Place the egg whites in a clean, greasefree bowl and whisk until soft peaks form, then gradually whisk in the sugar until stiff but not dry. Stir the egg yolks and melted chocolate together in a separate bowl, then stir in a little of the whisked egg whites. Gradually fold in the remaining egg whites.

4 Divide the mixture between the dishes. Bake in the preheated oven for 15 minutes, or until just set. Dust with cocoa powder and serve immediately with vanilla ice cream.

hot chocolate soufflé with coffee sabayon

🕚 **cook: 50 mins**   🕐 **prep: 25 mins**   **serves 4–6**

*Soufflés, especially chocolate ones, are not as tricky to make as is
often thought. The crucial point is to make sure that everyone is
sitting at the table when it is ready.*

variation

Replace the plain chocolate in the
soufflé with white chocolate and
serve with Chocolate Sauce (see
page 13) instead of the sabayon.

cook's tip

A prepared soufflé will keep in the
refrigerator for up to 2 hours before
cooking and will then still rise.

INGREDIENTS

butter, for greasing
55 g/2 oz golden caster sugar, plus
extra for coating
3 tbsp cornflour
250 ml/9 fl oz milk
115 g/4 oz plain chocolate,
broken into pieces
4 eggs, separated
icing sugar, for dusting

SABAYON

2 eggs
3 egg yolks
85 g/3 oz golden caster sugar
4 tsp instant coffee granules
2 tbsp brandy

1 Preheat the oven
to 190°C/375°F/Gas
Mark 5. Grease a 1-litre/1¾-pint
soufflé dish with butter and
coat with caster sugar. To make
the soufflé, place the cornflour
in a bowl. Add a little milk and
stir until smooth. Pour the
remaining milk into a heavy-
based saucepan and add the
chocolate. Heat gently until the
chocolate has melted, then stir.

Pour the chocolate milk on to
the cornflour paste, stirring.
Return to the pan and bring to
the boil, stirring. Simmer for
1 minute. Remove from the
heat and stir in the egg yolks,
one at a time, and the sugar.
Cover and cool slightly.

2 Place the egg whites in
a large, spotlessly clean,
greasefree bowl and whisk

until beginning to stand in soft
peaks. Gradually whisk in the
caster sugar until stiff but not
dry. Stir a little of the meringue
into the chocolate mixture,
then carefully fold in the
remainder. Pour into the
prepared soufflé dish and bake
in the preheated oven for 40
minutes, or until it
is well risen and wobbles
slightly when pushed.

3 Just before the soufflé
is ready, make the
coffee sabayon. Place all the
ingredients in a heavy-based
saucepan. Place the saucepan
over a very low heat and whisk
constantly, until the mixture
is thick and light. Dust a little
icing sugar over the soufflé
and serve immediately, with
the sabayon.

hot chocolate cheesecake

serves 8–10 **prep: 25 mins, plus 10 mins chilling** **cook: 1 hr 30 mins**

This rich and decadent cheesecake is doubly chocolatey, with chocolate in the pastry and the filling. It is delicious served warm.

INGREDIENTS

PASTRY

150 g/5½ oz plain flour, plus extra for dusting

2 tbsp cocoa powder

75 g/2¾ oz butter, diced, plus extra for greasing

2 tbsp golden caster sugar

25 g/1 oz ground almonds

1 egg yolk

FILLING

2 eggs, separated

75 g/2¾ oz golden caster sugar

350 g/12 oz cream cheese

40 g/1½ oz ground almonds

150 ml/5 fl oz double cream

25 g/1 oz cocoa powder, sifted

1 tsp vanilla essence

icing sugar, for dusting

variation

If you like, make a little extra pastry and use to form a lattice design on top of the filling, then bake as in main recipe.

cook's tip

To remove the cheesecake easily from the cake tin, stand the tin on top of a can and gently ease the sides down to the work surface, leaving the cheesecake on top of the can.

1 Preheat the oven to 160°C/325°F/Gas Mark 3. Grease a 20-cm/8-inch loose-bottomed cake tin with butter. To make the pastry, sift the flour and cocoa powder into a bowl. Add the butter and rub it in until the mixture resembles fine breadcrumbs. Stir in the sugar and almonds. Add the egg yolk and enough water to make a soft dough.

Roll out on a lightly floured work surface and use to line the tin. Chill in the refrigerator while preparing the filling.

2 To make the filling, place the egg yolks and caster sugar in a large bowl and whisk together until thick and pale. Whisk in the cheese, almonds, cream, cocoa powder and vanilla essence until blended.

3 Place the egg whites in a clean, greasefree bowl and whisk until stiff but not dry. Stir a little of the whisked egg whites into the cheese mixture, then fold in the remainder. Pour into the pastry case. Bake in the oven for 1½ hours, or until well risen and just firm to the touch. Remove from the tin and dust with icing sugar.

chocolate zabaglione

 cook: 5 mins   prep: 10 mins   serves 4

As this recipe only uses a little chocolate, choose one with a minimum of 70 per cent cocoa solids for a good flavour.

variation

For a change, substitute the Marsala wine for dry sherry or brandy and serve with sponge fingers instead of the amaretti biscuits.

cook's tip

Make the dessert just before serving as it will separate if left to stand. If it begins to curdle, remove it from the heat and place it in a bowl of cold water. Whisk furiously until the mixture comes together.

INGREDIENTS

4 egg yolks

4 tbsp caster sugar

50 g/1¾ oz plain chocolate

125 ml/4 fl oz Marsala wine

cocoa powder, for dusting

amaretti biscuits, to serve

1 Place the egg yolks and caster sugar in a large glass bowl and, using an electric whisk, whisk together until the mixture is very pale.

2 Grate the chocolate finely and, using a spatula, fold into the egg mixture. Fold the Marsala wine into the chocolate mixture.

3 Place the bowl over a saucepan of gently simmering water and set the electric whisk on the lowest speed or swap to a balloon whisk. Cook gently, whisking constantly, until the mixture thickens. Do not overcook or the mixture will curdle.

4 Spoon the hot mixture into 4 warmed glass dishes or coffee cups and dust with cocoa powder. Serve as soon as possible, while it is warm, light and fluffy, with amaretti biscuits.

gâteaux, cakes & tarts

Whether you are baking for a special occasion or just for family or friends, you can never fail to impress and satisfy with a chocolate cake or tart – it's practically everyone's favourite! So it's reassuring to know that you don't have to be an experienced or skilful cook to be able to produce such a crowd-pleaser whenever the fancy takes you or the need arises.

In this section, there are glorious gâteaux, such as Strawberry Chocolate Gâteau (see page 112) or Chocolate Truffle Torte (see page 115), which can be served as a dessert or for a celebration, or simpler family favourites, like Banana & Chocolate Teabread (see page 144) or Chocolate & Vanilla Marble Cake (see page 134). Also featured are some classic cakes from around the world, including Sicilian Cassata (see page 146) and the Viennese Sachertorte (see page 128), as well as delicious chocolate tarts, such as Chocolate Fudge Tart (see page 152) or tangy Lemon & Chocolate Tart (see page 150).

Whether your preference is for rich and creamy confections or plainer cakes with no more than a dusting of cocoa powder for decoration, there is something here to appeal to all tastes. One thing is for sure – whenever you have a chocolate cake nestling in the cake tin, it won't be there for long!

double chocolate roulade

serves 8

**prep: 30 mins, plus
10 hrs standing/chilling**

cook: 20–25 mins

*A dark chocolate mousse is rolled around white chocolate cream to
make a luscious dessert. Delicious served with summer berries.*

INGREDIENTS

4 eggs, separated

115 g/4 oz golden caster sugar

115 g/4 oz plain chocolate,

melted and cooled (see pages 9–10)

1 tsp instant coffee granules, dissolved

in 2 tbsp hot water, cooled

icing sugar, to decorate

cocoa powder, for dusting

fresh raspberries, to serve

FILLING

250 ml/9 fl oz whipping cream

140 g/5 oz white chocolate,

broken into pieces

3 tbsp Tia Maria

---

variation

If you like, replace the Tia Maria
with the same amount of brandy,
rum or orange juice.

---

cook's tip

If you do not have time, it is not
essential to chill the roulade for
2 hours before serving. However,
the roulade firms up in this time and
becomes easier to slice.

1 Preheat the oven to
180°C/350°F/Gas
Mark 4. Line a 23 x 33-cm/
9 x 13-inch Swiss roll tin with
non-stick baking paper. Whisk
the egg yolks and sugar in a
bowl until pale and mousse-
like. Fold in the chocolate,
then the coffee. Place the egg
whites in a clean bowl and
whisk until stiff but not dry.
Stir a little of the egg whites
into the chocolate mixture,
then fold in the remainder.
Pour into the tin and bake
for 15–20 minutes, or until
firm. Cover with a damp tea
towel and leave in the tin for
8 hours, or overnight.

2 Meanwhile, make the
filling. Heat the cream
until almost boiling. Place the
chocolate in a food processor
and chop roughly. With the
motor running, pour the cream
through the feed tube. Process
until smooth. Stir in the Tia
Maria. Transfer to a bowl
and cool. Chill for 8 hours,
or overnight.

3 To assemble the
roulade, whip the
chocolate cream until soft
peaks form. Cut a sheet of
greaseproof paper larger than
the roulade, place on a work
surface and sift icing sugar over
it. Turn the roulade out on to
the paper. Peel away the lining
paper. Spread the chocolate
cream over the roulade and roll
up from the short side nearest
to you. Transfer to a serving
dish, seam-side down. Chill for
2 hours, then dust with cocoa
powder. Serve with raspberries.

raspberry dessert cake

serves 8–10   **prep: 20 mins, plus** 🕑 **15 mins cooling**   **cook: 40–50 mins** 🕑

The raspberries in this luxurious dark chocolate cake give it a fresh, tangy flavour. Serve with fresh raspberries and whipped cream.

INGREDIENTS

225 g/8 oz butter, plus extra
for greasing
250 g/9 oz plain chocolate,
broken into pieces
1 tbsp strong dark coffee
5 eggs
85 g/3 oz golden caster sugar
85 g/3 oz plain flour
1 tsp ground cinnamon
175 g/6 oz fresh raspberries
icing sugar, for dusting

TO SERVE
fresh raspberries
whipped cream

---

variation

If fresh raspberries are not available, frozen raspberries may be used. Since these will be softer than fresh fruit, take care to thaw them thoroughly and drain off any excess juice.

1 Preheat the oven to 160°C/325°F/Gas Mark 3. Grease a 23-cm/9-inch cake tin with butter and line the base with baking paper. Place the chocolate, butter and coffee in a small heatproof bowl and set over a saucepan of gently simmering water until melted. Stir, then remove from the heat and cool slightly.

2 Place the eggs and sugar in a separate bowl and beat together until thick and pale. Gently fold in the chocolate mixture. Sift the flour and ground cinnamon into a separate bowl, then fold into the chocolate mixture. Pour into the prepared tin and sprinkle the raspberries evenly over the top.

3 Bake in the hot oven for 35–45 minutes, or until the cake is well risen and springy to the touch. Leave to cool in the tin for 15 minutes before turning out on to a large serving plate. Dust with icing sugar before serving with fresh raspberries and cream.

chocolate & mango layer

cook: 1 hr 10 mins

prep: 30 mins, plus 1 hr cooling

serves 12

Canned peaches can be used instead of mangoes for this deliciously moist cake, if you prefer.

cook's tip

It is very important that the cream is only lightly whipped as it thickens when the cooled chocolate is added. Use a rubber spatula to fold the chocolate in gently.

INGREDIENTS

butter, for greasing

50 g/1¾ oz cocoa powder

150 ml/5 fl oz boiling water

6 large eggs

350 g/12 oz caster sugar

300 g/10½ oz self-raising flour

800 g/1 lb 12 oz canned mangoes

1 tsp cornflour

425 ml/15 fl oz double cream

75 g/2¾ oz plain chocolate, grated

1 Preheat the oven to 160°C/325°F/Gas Mark 3. Grease and line a deep 23-cm/9-inch round cake tin. Place the cocoa powder in a small, heatproof bowl, gradually add the boiling water and blend until smooth.

2 Whisk the eggs and caster sugar together until light and foamy and the whisk leaves a trail that lasts a few seconds when lifted. Fold in the cocoa mixture. Sift the flour and fold into the mixture, then pour into the tin and smooth the top. Bake in the hot oven for 1 hour, or until springy to the touch. Cool in the tin for 5 minutes, then turn out on to a wire rack and cool completely. Peel off the paper and cut the cake into 3 layers.

3 Drain the mangoes, reserving the juice. Place one-quarter of them in a blender and purée until smooth. Mix the cornflour with 3 tablespoons of the juice to form a paste, then add to the mango purée. Transfer to a saucepan and heat, stirring, until thick. Cool. Chop the remaining mango. Whip the cream and reserve one-quarter.

Fold the mango into the remaining cream and use to sandwich the layers of cake together. Place on a serving plate. Spread some of the remaining cream around the side of the cake, then press the grated chocolate into the cream. Spread the mango purée over the centre and pipe cream rosettes around the top.

strawberry chocolate gâteau

cook: 30–40 mins   **prep: 25 mins**   **serves 8**

*Fresh strawberries and whipped cream with light chocolate sponge
make the perfect treat for a hot summer's day.*

variation

If you like, replace the kirsch with
another liqueur, such as Cointreau,
or use brandy instead.

cook's tip

If you do not want to make
the Chocolate Curls, either use the
ready-made variety or decorate the
side of the cake with crushed
chocolate flake bars.

INGREDIENTS

SPONGE

butter, for greasing

3 eggs

115 g/4 oz golden caster sugar

90 g/3¼ oz self-raising flour

2 tbsp cocoa powder

FILLING AND TOPPING

250 g/9 oz strawberries

300 ml/10 fl oz double cream

½ tsp vanilla essence

1 tbsp icing sugar

2 tbsp kirsch

Chocolate Curls (see page 10)

1 Preheat the oven to 190°C/375°F/Gas Mark 5. Grease and line a 22-cm/8½-inch cake tin. To make the sponge, place the eggs and sugar in a bowl and whisk until thick and mousse-like and a trail is left when the whisk is lifted. Sift the flour and cocoa powder into a separate bowl, then fold into the whisked mixture. Turn into the tin and bake in the oven for 30–40 minutes, or until the cake springs back when pressed in the centre. Leave in the tin for 5 minutes, then turn out on to a wire rack to cool.

2 Meanwhile, prepare the filling. Reserve 4 strawberries and hull and slice the remainder. Whip the cream, vanilla essence and icing sugar together until thick. Reserve two-thirds of the cream and fold the strawberries into the remainder.

3 Slice the sponge horizontally into 2 layers and sprinkle each layer with 1 tablespoon of kirsch. Place one layer on a serving plate and spread over the strawberry cream mixture. Place the other sponge layer on top. Place some of the reserved cream mixture in a piping bag fitted with a fluted nozzle and spread the remainder over the top and sides of the cake. Coat the sides with Chocolate Curls. Pipe the cream round the top of the cake. Cut the reserved strawberries in half, keeping the stalks intact, and arrange on the piped cream.

orange mousse cake

serves 12

prep: 20 mins, plus 1 hr ⟲
30 mins cooling/chilling

cook: 40 mins ⟲

With a dark chocolate sponge sandwiched together with a light, creamy orange mousse, this spectacular cake is irresistible.

INGREDIENTS

175 g/6 oz butter

175 g/6 oz caster sugar

4 eggs, lightly beaten

1 tbsp cocoa powder

200 g/7 oz self-raising flour

50 g/1¾ oz orange-flavoured chocolate

MOUSSE

2 eggs, separated

4 tbsp caster sugar

200 ml/7 fl oz orange juice

2 tsp gelatine

300 ml/10 fl oz double cream

peeled orange slices, to decorate

cook's tip

For best results and a real orange taste, use plain orange-flavoured chocolate for the sponge and freshly squeezed orange juice in the mousse.

1 Preheat the oven to 180°C/350°F/Gas Mark 4. Grease and line the base of a 20-cm/8-inch springform cake tin. Beat the butter and sugar in a bowl until light and fluffy. Gradually add the eggs, beating well after each addition. Sift the cocoa powder and flour together and fold into the mixture. Fold in the chocolate.

2 Pour into the tin and smooth the top. Bake for 40 minutes, or until springy to the touch. Leave in the tin for 5 minutes, then turn out and cool on a wire rack. Cut the cold cake into 2 layers.

3 To make the mousse. Beat the egg yolks and sugar together until light, then whisk in the orange juice. Place

3 tablespoons of cold water in a bowl and sprinkle the gelatine over the top. Leave for 5 minutes, or until spongy, then place over a saucepan of hot water and stir until dissolved. Stir into the mousse.

4 Whip the cream until just holding its shape, reserve a little for decoration and fold the rest into the

mousse. Whisk the egg whites in a clean bowl until soft peaks form, then fold into the mousse. Leave in a cool place until beginning to set, stirring occasionally. Place half the cake in the tin. Pour in the mousse and press the second cake layer on top. Chill until set. Transfer to a serving dish, pipe cream rosettes on the top and arrange orange slices in the centre.

chocolate truffle torte

⏱ **cook: 7–10 mins**   ⏳ **prep: 40 mins, plus 4–5 hrs chilling**   **serves 10**

Chocolate and cream on a thin sponge base make this a wickedly rich dessert for an extra special occasion.

cook's tip

Dip the blade of your knife in hot water before slicing the torte – this will prevent torte sticking to it or crumbling.

INGREDIENTS

butter, for greasing

55 g/2 oz golden caster sugar

2 eggs

25 g/1 oz plain flour

25 g/1 oz cocoa powder, plus

extra to decorate

50 ml/2 fl oz cold strong black coffee

2 tbsp brandy

FILLING

600 ml/1 pint whipping cream

425 g/15 oz plain chocolate, melted

and cooled (see pages 9–10)

icing sugar, to decorate

1 Preheat the oven to 220°C/425°F/Gas Mark 7. Grease a 23-cm/9-inch springform cake tin with butter and line the base with baking paper. Place the sugar and eggs in a heatproof bowl and set over a saucepan of hot water. Whisk together until pale and mousse-like. Sift the flour and cocoa powder into a separate bowl, then fold gently into the mixture. Pour into the prepared tin and bake in the preheated oven for 7–10 minutes, or until risen and firm to the touch.

2 Transfer to a wire rack to cool. Wash and dry the tin and replace the cooled cake in the tin. Mix the coffee and brandy together and brush over the cake. To make the filling, place the cream in a bowl and whip until very soft peaks form. Carefully fold in the cooled chocolate. Pour the chocolate mixture over the sponge. Leave to chill in the refrigerator for 4–5 hours, or until set.

3 To decorate the torte, sift cocoa powder over the top and remove carefully from the tin. Using strips of card or greaseproof paper, sift bands of icing sugar over the torte to create a striped pattern. Serve.

mocha layer cake

serves 8   prep: 20 mins, plus ↻   cook: 35–45 mins ⏱
30 mins cooling

*Chocolate cake and a creamy coffee-flavoured filling are combined
in this delicious mocha cake. Serve with afternoon tea.*

INGREDIENTS

butter for greasing

200 g/7 oz self-raising flour

¼ tsp baking powder

4 tbsp cocoa powder

100 g/3½ oz caster sugar

2 eggs

2 tbsp golden syrup

150 ml/5 fl oz sunflower oil

150 ml/5 fl oz milk

FILLING

1 tsp instant coffee

1 tbsp boiling water

300 ml/10 fl oz double cream

2 tbsp icing sugar

TO DECORATE

50 g/1¾ oz plain grated chocolate

Chocolate Caraque (see page 10)

icing sugar, for dusting

---

variation

Replace the plain grated chocolate
with chopped nuts. Alternatively
arrange Chocolate Leaves around the
edge (see page 11).

---

cook's tip

To test that the cake is cooked, lightly
press the centre with your fingertips –
if it springs back, then it is done.
Remove from the oven and cool in the
tin for 5 minutes, then cool completely
on a wire rack.

1 Preheat the oven to 180°C/350°F/Gas Mark 4. Lightly grease 3 x 18-cm/7-inch cake tins.

2 Sift the flour, baking powder and cocoa powder into a large bowl, then stir in the sugar. Make a well in the centre and stir in the eggs, syrup, sunflower oil and milk. Beat with a wooden spoon, gradually mixing in the dry ingredients to make a smooth batter. Divide the mixture between the tins.

3 Bake in the preheated oven for 35–45 minutes, or until springy to the touch. Leave in the tins for 5 minutes, then turn out and leave to cool completely on a wire rack.

4 To make the filling, dissolve the instant coffee in the boiling water and place in a large bowl with the cream and icing sugar. Whip until the cream is just holding its shape, then use half the cream to sandwich the 3 cakes together. Spread the remaining cream over the top and sides of the cake. Press the grated chocolate into the cream around the edge of the cake. Transfer the cake to a serving plate. Lay the Chocolate Caraque over the top of the cake. Cut a few thin strips of baking paper and place on top of the Chocolate Caraque. Dust lightly with icing sugar, then carefully remove the paper. Serve.

double chocolate gâteau

cook: 55–65 mins   **prep: 1 hr, plus 2 hrs chilling**   serves 10

This chocolate sponge layered with white chocolate cream and covered in dark chocolate icing could be served either as a celebration cake or a dessert.

variation

Mix 115 g/4 oz fresh raspberries to the whipped cream and use to fill the gâteau. Omit the chocolate, if you like and serve with raspberries.

cook's tip

It is important to use the correct cake tin as it will affect the baking time and the finished cake, so always use the type that is specified in the recipe.

INGREDIENTS

butter, for greasing

FILLING

250 ml/9 fl oz whipping cream

225 g/8 oz white chocolate, broken into pieces

SPONGE

225 g/8 oz butter, softened

225 g/8 oz golden caster sugar

4 eggs, beaten

175 g/6 oz self-raising flour

55 g/2 oz cocoa powder

1–2 tbsp milk (optional)

ICING

350 g/12 oz plain chocolate, broken into pieces

115 g/4 oz butter

85 ml/3 fl oz double cream

TO DECORATE

Chocolate Curls (see page 10), chilled

115 g/4 oz plain chocolate, broken into pieces

2 tsp icing sugar and cocoa powder, mixed together

1 Grease and line the base of a 20-cm/8-inch deep round cake tin. To make the filling, heat the cream to almost boiling. Place the white chocolate in a blender and chop roughly. With the motor running, pour the cream through the feed tube. Blend for 10–15 seconds, or until the mixture is smooth. Transfer to a bowl and cool. Cover and chill for 2 hours, or until firm. Whisk until just beginning to hold soft peaks.

2 Preheat the oven to 180°C/350°F/Gas Mark 4. To make the sponge, beat the butter and sugar together until light and fluffy. Gradually beat in the eggs. Sift the flour and cocoa powder into a separate bowl, then fold into the mixture, adding a little milk, if necessary, to make a dropping consistency. Spoon into the tin, smooth the surface and bake in the oven for 45–50 minutes, or until springy to the touch and a skewer inserted into the centre comes out clean. Leave the sponge in the tin for 5 minutes, then turn out on to a wire rack to cool.

3 To make the icing, melt the chocolate (see pages 9–10). Stir in the butter and cream. Cool, stirring frequently, until the mixture is a thick, spreading consistency. Slice the cake into 3 layers. Sandwich the layers together with the filling. Cover the top and sides with icing, place Chocolate Curls on top and sift the icing sugar and cocoa over the cake.

dark & white chocolate torte

serves 6   **prep: 20 mins, plus 1 hr** ⏲ **20 mins cooling/setting**   **cook: 35–40 mins** ⏲

If you can't decide if you prefer bitter dark chocolate or rich, creamy white chocolate then this gâteau is for you.

INGREDIENTS

butter, for greasing

4 eggs

100 g/3½ oz caster sugar

100 g/3½ oz plain flour

FILLING

300 ml/10 fl oz double cream

150 g/5½ oz plain chocolate, broken into small pieces

TOPPING

75 g/2¾ oz white chocolate

1 tbsp butter

1 tbsp milk

4 tbsp icing sugar

cook's tip

Add the finishing touch to this wonderful gâteau by decorating it with Chocolate Caraque (see page 10). Use plain or white chocolate for the curls or a mixture of both.

1 Preheat the oven to 180°C/350°F/Gas Mark 4. Grease and line the base of a 20-cm/8-inch round springform cake tin. Place the eggs and caster sugar in a large bowl and, using an electric whisk, whisk for 10 minutes, or until very light and foamy and the whisk leaves a trail that lasts a few seconds when lifted.

2 Sift the flour and fold in with a metal spoon or spatula. Pour into the prepared tin and bake in the hot oven for 35–40 minutes, or until springy to the touch. Leave to cool slightly, then transfer to a wire rack to cool completely.

3 To make the filling, place the cream in a saucepan and bring to the boil, stirring. Add the chocolate and stir until melted. Remove from the heat, transfer to a bowl and cool. Beat until thick.

4 Slice the cold cake into 2 layers, then sandwich the layers together with the cream. Place on a wire rack.

5 To make the topping, place the chocolate and butter in a small heatproof bowl and set over a saucepan of simmering water until melted. Stir until blended. Remove from the heat and whisk in the milk, then sift in the icing sugar. Continue whisking for a few minutes until the icing is cool. Pour it over the cake and spread with a spatula to coat the top and sides. Leave to set, then serve.

devil's food cake

cook: 30 mins

prep: 20 mins, plus 1 hr cooling

serves 10–12

This is an American classic, consisting of a rich, melt-in-the-mouth chocolate cake that has a delicious citrus-flavoured icing.

variation

For a touch of decadence, replace the citrus-flavoured icing with a Chocolate Fudge Icing (see page 122) and serve with fresh berries.

INGREDIENTS

225 g/8 oz butter, plus extra for greasing

100 g/3½ oz plain chocolate

250 g/9 oz self-raising flour

1 tsp bicarbonate of soda

400 g/14 oz dark muscovado sugar

1 tsp vanilla essence

3 eggs

125 ml/4 fl oz buttermilk

ICING

300 g/10½ oz caster sugar

2 egg whites

1 tbsp lemon juice

3 tbsp orange juice

candied orange peel, to decorate

1 Preheat the oven to 190°C/375°F/Gas Mark 5. Lightly grease and line the bases of 2 x 20-cm/8-inch shallow round cake tins. Melt the chocolate (see pages 9–10). Sift the flour and bicarbonate of soda together.

2 Place the butter and sugar in a large bowl and beat until pale and fluffy.

Beat in the vanilla essence and the eggs, one at a time, beating well after each addition. Add a little flour if the mixture begins to curdle.

3 Fold the melted chocolate into the mixture until well blended. Fold in the remaining flour, then stir in the buttermilk and 225 ml/8 fl oz boiling water.

4 Divide the mixture between the tins and smooth the tops. Bake in the hot oven for 30 minutes, or until springy to the touch. Cool in the tin for 5 minutes, then transfer to a wire rack and leave to cool completely.

5 Place the icing ingredients in a large bowl set over a saucepan of

simmering water. Using an electric whisk, whisk until thick and forming soft peaks. Remove from the heat and whisk until the mixture is cool.

6 Sandwich the 2 cakes together with a little of the icing, then spread the remainder over the sides and top of the cake. Decorate with candied orange peel.

chocolate fudge cake

serves 8

prep: 25 mins, plus ⟲
2 hrs cooling/chilling

cook: 35–45 mins ⟳

This opulent chocolate cake with a rich, soft fudgy icing
makes the perfect birthday cake for a chocolate-lover.

INGREDIENTS

175 g/6 oz unsalted butter, softened,
plus extra for greasing

175 g/6 oz golden caster sugar

3 eggs, beaten

3 tbsp golden syrup

40 g/1½ oz ground almonds

175 g/6 oz self-raising flour

pinch of salt

40 g/1½ oz cocoa powder

ICING

225 g/8 oz plain chocolate,
broken into pieces

55 g/2 oz dark muscovado sugar

225 g/8 oz unsalted butter, diced

5 tbsp evaporated milk

½ tsp vanilla essence

variation

To make the icing really creamy,
replace the evaporated milk with
the same amount of single cream.

cook's tip

Beat the eggs into the butter and
sugar one at a time, and beat well
after each addition. If the cake mixture
begins to curdle while you are adding
the eggs, beat in a little of the flour.

1 Grease and line the
base of 2 x 20-cm/
8-inch cake tins. To make the
icing, place the chocolate,
sugar, butter, evaporated milk
and vanilla essence in a heavy-
based saucepan. Heat gently,
stirring constantly, until
melted. Pour into a bowl and
leave to cool. Cover and chill
in the refrigerator for 1 hour,
or until spreadable.

2 Preheat the oven to
180°C/350°F/Gas
Mark 4. Place the butter and
sugar in a bowl and beat
together until light and fluffy.
Gradually beat in the eggs. Stir
in the syrup and ground
almonds. Sift the flour, salt and
cocoa powder into a separate
bowl, then fold into the
mixture. Add a little water, if
necessary, to make a dropping

consistency. Spoon the
mixture into the prepared
tins and bake in the oven for
30–35 minutes, or until springy
to the touch and a skewer
inserted in the centre comes
out clean.

3 Leave the cakes in the
tins for 5 minutes, then
turn out on to wire racks to
cool completely. When the

cakes are cold, sandwich them
together with half the icing.
Spread the remaining icing
over the top and sides of the
cake, swirling it to give a
frosted appearance.

chocolate cake with coffee syrup

cook: 50 mins   **prep: 15 mins**   **serves 12**

*An intensely flavoured chocolate cake that is particularly good
served slightly warm, with crème fraîche, as a dessert.*

variation

Split the cake in half horizontally
and fill the centre with whipped
cream and stoned morello cherries,
then serve with the coffee syrup.

cook's tip

When making syrups, keep a pastry
brush and a jug of cold water nearby
to brush the sides of the saucepan
occasionally with water. This helps to
prevent crystallization.

INGREDIENTS

115 g/4 oz unsalted butter,
plus extra for greasing
225 g/8 oz plain chocolate,
broken into pieces
1 tbsp strong black coffee
4 large eggs
2 egg yolks
115 g/4 oz golden caster sugar
55 g/2 oz plain flour
2 tsp ground cinnamon
50 g/1¾ oz ground almonds
chocolate-covered coffee beans,
to decorate

SYRUP

300 ml/10 fl oz strong black coffee
115 g/4 oz golden caster sugar
1 cinnamon stick

1 Preheat the oven
to 190°C/375°F/Gas
Mark 5. Grease and line the
base of a deep 20-cm/8-inch
round cake tin. Place the
chocolate, butter and coffee
in a heatproof bowl and set
over a saucepan of gently
simmering water until melted.
Stir to blend, then remove
from the heat and leave to
cool slightly.

2 Place the whole eggs,
egg yolks and sugar in
a separate bowl and whisk
together until thick and pale.
Sift the flour and cinnamon
over the egg mixture. Add the
almonds and the chocolate
mixture and fold in carefully.
Spoon the mixture into the
prepared tin. Bake in the oven
for 35 minutes, or until a
skewer inserted into the centre

comes out clean. Leave to cool
slightly before turning out on
to a serving plate.

3 Meanwhile, make the
syrup. Place the coffee,
sugar and cinnamon stick
in a heavy-based saucepan and
heat gently, stirring, until the
sugar has dissolved. Increase
the heat and boil for 5
minutes, or until reduced and

thickened slightly. Keep warm.
Pierce the surface of the cake
with a skewer, then drizzle over
half the coffee syrup. Decorate
with chocolate-covered coffee
beans and serve, cut into
wedges, with the remaining
coffee syrup.

chocolate passion cake

serves 6   prep: 25 mins, plus 🕐 1 hr cooling   cook: 45 mins 🕐

What could be nicer than passion cake with added chocolate? Rich and moist, this cake is fabulous with afternoon tea.

INGREDIENTS

butter, for greasing

5 eggs

150 g/5½ oz caster sugar

150 g/5½ oz plain flour

40 g/1½ oz cocoa powder

175 g/6 oz carrots, peeled, finely grated and squeezed until dry

50 g/1¾ oz chopped walnuts

2 tbsp sunflower oil

350 g/12 oz medium-fat soft cheese

175 g/6 oz icing sugar

175 g/6 oz milk or plain chocolate, melted (see pages 9–10)

cook's tip

The undecorated cake can be frozen for up to 2 months. Thaw at room temperature for 3 hours or preferably overnight in the refrigerator.

1   Preheat the oven to 190°C/375°F/Gas Mark 5. Lightly grease and line the base of a 20-cm/8-inch deep round cake tin.

2   Place the eggs and sugar in a large heatproof bowl set over a saucepan of gently simmering water and, using an electric whisk, whisk until very thick and the whisk leaves a trail that lasts a few seconds when lifted.

3   Remove the bowl from the heat. Sift the flour and cocoa powder into the bowl and carefully fold in. Fold in the carrots, walnuts and sunflower oil until the mixture is just blended.

4   Pour into the prepared tin and bake in the preheated oven for 45 minutes. Leave to cool slightly, then turn out on to a wire rack to cool completely.

5   Beat the soft cheese and icing sugar together until blended, then beat in the melted chocolate. Split the cake in half and sandwich together again with half the chocolate mixture. Cover the top of the cake with the remainder of the chocolate mixture, swirling it with a knife. Leave to chill in the refrigerator until required or serve immediately.

caribbean chocolate cake

cook: 45–50 mins   **prep: 10 mins, plus 1 hr 20 mins cooling/setting**   **serves 12**

Chocolate and spice are combined in this light cake, which has a tasty stem ginger topping and is perfect for any time of the day.

cook's tip

If possible, this cake benefits from being kept in an airtight container for a day before eating, although it might not last that long.

INGREDIENTS

115 g/4 oz butter, plus extra
for greasing
200 g/7 oz self-raising flour
25 g/1 oz cocoa powder
1 tbsp ground ginger
1 tsp ground cinnamon
½ tsp bicarbonate of soda
115 g/4 oz light muscovado sugar
2 eggs
1½ tbsp golden syrup
1½ tbsp milk
6 pieces stem ginger, plus ginger syrup
from the jar
115 g/4 oz icing sugar
1 tbsp rum

1 Preheat the oven to 160°C/325°F/Gas Mark 3. Grease and line the base of a shallow 18-cm/ 7-inch square cake tin. Sift the flour, cocoa powder, ground ginger, cinnamon and bicarbonate of soda into a large bowl. Add the butter and rub it in with your fingertips, then stir in the sugar. Make a well in the centre.

2 Place the eggs in a separate bowl with the syrup and milk. Whisk together, then pour into the dry ingredients and beat until smooth and glossy. Spoon the mixture into the tin. Bake for 45–50 minutes, or until well risen and firm to the touch. Leave in the tin for 30 minutes, then turn out on to a wire rack to cool completely.

3 Cut each piece of stem ginger into quarters and arrange on top of the cake. Sift the icing sugar into a bowl and stir in the rum and enough of the ginger syrup to make a smooth icing. Drizzle the icing over the cake and leave to set. Cut the cake into 12 squares to serve.

sachertorte

serves 8–10

prep: 25 mins, plus ⏲ 2 hrs setting

cook: 1 hr 10 mins– 1 hr 25 mins ⏲

Sachertorte is a most famous Viennese speciality with a distinctive glazed finish. It is the perfect cake for a very special occasion.

INGREDIENTS

115 g/4 oz unsalted butter, softened, plus extra for greasing

175 g/6 oz plain chocolate, broken into pieces

3 tbsp black coffee

140 g/5 oz golden caster sugar

5 eggs, separated

140 g/5 oz plain flour, sifted

4 tbsp apricot jam

dash of lemon juice

1 tbsp water

ICING

85 g/3 oz golden caster sugar

4 tbsp water

100 g/3½ oz plain chocolate, broken into pieces

variation

If making this cake for a special occasion, serve with fresh fruit. If apricot jam is unavailable, you can use raspberry jam instead.

cook's tip

The traditional glaze on this cake can be quite tricky. An easier method is to melt 175 g/6 oz plain chocolate and 2 tablespoons single cream together, then spread over the cake and leave to set.

1 Preheat the oven to 160°C/325°F/Gas Mark 3. Grease and line a 23-cm/9-inch round cake tin. Heat the chocolate in a pan with the coffee until melted, stir and cool. Beat the butter and 85 g/3 oz of the sugar in a bowl until fluffy. Beat in the chocolate mixture and egg yolks. Stir in the flour. Whisk the egg whites in a separate

bowl until stiff. Whisk in the remaining sugar. Fold into the cake mixture. Turn into the tin and bake for 1–1¼ hours, until firm. Leave in the tin for 5 minutes. Turn out to cool.

2 Slice the cake in half horizontally. Sandwich together with half the jam. Heat the remaining jam, lemon juice and water in a pan until

the jam has melted. Sieve into a bowl. Brush the jam over the top and sides of the cake.

3 For the icing, heat the sugar and water until boiling and stir until the sugar has dissolved. Remove from the heat, add the chocolate and stir until smooth. Return to the heat and boil to a temperature of 116°C/241°F on

a sugar thermometer. Remove from the heat, stir until the mixture stops bubbling, then pour all but 2 tablespoons quickly over the top of the cake, letting it flow down the sides. Smooth round the sides, but do not touch the top. When the icing begins to set, warm the reserved icing and drip the 'Sacher' signature over the top from the tip of a knife.

yule log

cook: 16–18 mins   **prep: 35 mins, plus 30 mins cooling**   **serves 8**

A chocolate yule log is a popular alternative to a Christmas cake and makes an eye-catching centrepiece for a festive table.

variation

Replace the Cointreau with brandy, or if you do not want to use any alcohol, use orange juice instead.

cook's tip

To roll the sponge, wring out a tea towel with hot water and place on a work surface. Place greaseproof paper on top, sprinkled with caster sugar. Put the sponge on top, peel off the lining paper and roll up from a long side.

INGREDIENTS

butter, for greasing

3 eggs

115 g/4 oz golden caster sugar

55 g/2 oz plain flour

25 g/1 oz cocoa powder, plus extra for dusting

Chocolate Caraque (see page 10)

55 g/2 oz white chocolate, melted (see pages 9–10)

icing sugar, for dusting

SYRUP

55 g/2 oz golden caster sugar

150 ml/5 fl oz water

4 tbsp Cointreau

ICING

55 g/2 oz butter, softened

115 g/4 oz icing sugar, sifted

grated rind of 1 orange

1 tbsp Cointreau

BUTTERCREAM

1 tbsp cocoa powder

1 tbsp boiling water

85 g/3 oz butter

175 g/6 oz icing sugar, sifted

1 Preheat the oven to 200°C/400°F/Gas Mark 6. Grease and line a 20 x 30-cm/8 x 12-inch Swiss roll tin. Whisk the eggs and sugar together until thick and a trail is left when the whisk is lifted. Sift the flour and cocoa powder together into a separate bowl, then fold into the egg mixture. Turn into the tin and bake for 8–10 minutes, or until the cake springs back when lightly pressed. Roll up the sponge (see Cook's Tip) and leave to cool.

2 To make the syrup, heat the sugar and water in a pan until the sugar dissolves. Boil for 2 minutes. Stir in the Cointreau and cool. Unroll the sponge and remove the paper. Sprinkle the sponge with syrup. To make the icing, beat the butter until creamy. Beat in the other ingredients until smooth. Spread over the sponge and roll up.

3 To make the buttercream, place the cocoa in a heatproof bowl and stir in the water. Cool. Beat the butter in a separate bowl until creamy. Gradually beat in the icing sugar and cocoa until smooth. Cut off a quarter of the roll diagonally and attach to the side of the roll with buttercream. Cover the roll with buttercream and mark lines to represent bark. Cover with Chocolate Caraque. Pipe white chocolate spirals on to the ends. Dust with cocoa and icing sugar and serve.

german chocolate & hazelnut cake

serves 8 **prep: 10 mins, plus 30 mins cooling** **cook: 45–50 mins**

This is a classic German cake that tastes wonderful served as an afternoon snack with a hot cup of coffee or tea.

INGREDIENTS

175 g/6 oz unsalted butter, softened, plus extra for greasing

115 g/4 oz self-raising flour, plus extra for dusting

175 g/6 oz dark muscovado sugar

1 tbsp cocoa powder

1 tsp mixed spice

3 eggs, beaten

115 g/4 oz ground hazelnuts

2 tbsp black coffee

icing sugar, for dusting

cook's tip

A kugelhopf tin is a special fluted ring tin, available from specialist kitchen shops. If you do not have one, you can use a 23-cm/9-inch ring mould instead.

1 Preheat the oven to 180°C/350°F/Gas Mark 4. Grease and flour a 19-cm/7½-inch kugelhopf tin. Place the butter and muscovado sugar in a large bowl and beat together until light and fluffy. Sift the self-raising flour, cocoa powder and mixed spice into a separate bowl.

2 Beat the eggs into the creamed mixture, one at a time, adding 1 tablespoon of the flour mixture with the second and third eggs. Fold in the remaining flour mixture, ground hazelnuts and coffee.

3 Turn into the prepared tin and bake in the hot oven for 45–50 minutes, or until the cake springs back when lightly pressed. Leave in the tin for 10 minutes, then turn out on to a wire rack to cool completely. Dust generously with icing sugar before serving.

orange & chocolate ring cake

⏱ **cook: 40 mins**   ⏲ **prep: 25 mins, plus 1 hr cooling/setting**   **serves 8–10**

The addition of fresh oranges makes this cake very fruity and moist. It will be an instant favourite with friends and family.

cook's tip

You need not be skilful to ice a cake in this way – the more 'spontaneous' it looks, the better! Just drizzle the icing over the cake, then drizzle the chocolate over the top.

INGREDIENTS

175 g/6 oz butter, softened,
plus extra for greasing

2 small oranges

85 g/3 oz plain chocolate

200 g/7 oz self-raising flour

1½ tsp baking powder

175 g/6 oz golden caster sugar

3 eggs, beaten

GLAZE

225 g/8 oz icing sugar

2 tbsp orange juice

55 g/2 oz plain chocolate,
broken into pieces

1 Preheat the oven to 160°C/325°F/Gas Mark 3. Thoroughly grease an 850-ml/1½-pint fluted or plain ring mould. Grate the rind of 1 orange and reserve. Remove the rind of the other orange in fine strips with a zester and reserve. Cut the skin and pith from the oranges, then cut them into segments by cutting down between the membranes with a sharp knife. Chop the segments into small pieces, reserving as much juice as possible. Grate the chocolate on to a plate.

2 Sift the flour and baking powder into a large bowl. Add the butter, sugar, eggs, grated orange rind and any reserved juice. Beat until smooth. Gently fold in the chopped oranges and grated chocolate. Spoon the mixture into the tin. Bake in the oven for 40 minutes, or until well risen and golden brown. Leave in the tin for 5 minutes, then turn out on to a wire rack and cool completely.

3 To make the glaze, sift the icing sugar into a bowl and stir in enough orange juice to make a coating consistency. Using a spoon, drizzle the icing over the cake. Melt the chocolate (see pages 9–10) and drizzle over the cake. Sprinkle the reserved strips of orange rind on top. Leave to set before serving.

chocolate & vanilla marble cake

serves 10   **prep: 25 mins, plus** ⏱
1 hr cooling/setting   **cook: 1 hr–1 hr 10 mins** ⏲

*This cake looks impressive but it is easy to make. Just drag a
skewer through two contrasting cake mixtures to create a
professional-looking marbled effect.*

INGREDIENTS

225 g/8 oz butter, softened,
plus extra for greasing

55 g/2 oz plain chocolate,
broken into pieces

1 tbsp strong black coffee

225 g/8 oz self-raising flour

1 tsp baking powder

225 g/8 oz golden caster sugar

4 eggs, beaten

55 g/2 oz ground almonds

2 tbsp milk

1 tsp vanilla essence

ICING

125 g/4½ oz plain chocolate,
broken into pieces

25 g/1 oz butter

2 tbsp water

variation

If you don't have a ring mould, you
can use a 23-cm/9-inch deep round
cake tin instead. Replace the icing
with a Fudge Sauce (see page 161).

cook's tip

If you would prefer a plainer cake,
omit the chocolate icing and simply
dust the top of the cake with sifted
icing sugar before serving.

1 Preheat the oven
to 180°C/350°F/Gas
Mark 4. Grease a 1.7-litre/
3-pint ring mould. Place the
chocolate and coffee in a
heatproof bowl and set over a
saucepan of gently simmering
water until the chocolate has
melted. Stir until smooth and
leave to cool. Sift the flour and
baking powder into a separate

bowl. Add the butter, sugar,
eggs, ground almonds and
milk. Beat together thoroughly
until smooth.

2 Transfer one half of
the mixture to another
bowl and stir in the vanilla
essence. Stir the melted
chocolate into the other half
of the mixture. Place spoonfuls

of the 2 mixtures alternately
into the prepared mould, then
drag a skewer through to
create a marbled effect.
Smooth the top. Bake in the
oven for 50–60 minutes, or
until well risen and a skewer
inserted into the centre comes
out clean. Leave in the tin for 5
minutes, then turn out on to a
wire rack to cool completely.

3 To make the icing, place
the chocolate, butter
and water in a heatproof bowl
and set over a saucepan of
simmering water until melted.
Stir until smooth, then pour
over the cake, working quickly
to coat the top and sides.
Leave to set before serving.

sunken drunken chocolate cake

🍳 cook: 40–45 mins   🕐 prep: 15 mins, plus 30 mins cooling   serves 8–10

This dense, rich cake contains no flour and will sink and crack slightly when you take it out of the oven.

variation

Serve as a dessert with vanilla ice cream or fresh fruit such as strawberries and sliced peaches.

cook's tip

This cake is very fragile and benefits from being chilled for at least 10 minutes in the refrigerator before serving. Any uneaten cake should be covered with foil and stored in the refrigerator.

INGREDIENTS

115 g/4 oz butter, diced, plus extra for greasing

flour, for dusting

140 g/5 oz plain chocolate, broken into pieces

2 tbsp brandy

85 g/3 oz golden caster sugar

6 eggs, separated

140 g/5 oz ground almonds

425 ml/15 fl oz whipped cream, to decorate

ground cinnamon, for dusting

1 Preheat the oven to 160°C/325°F/Gas Mark 3. Grease a 23-cm/9-inch springform cake tin and line the base with non-stick baking paper. Dust the sides with flour. Place the chocolate and brandy in a heatproof bowl and set over a saucepan of simmering water until the chocolate has melted. Stir until smooth, then cool slightly.

2 Place the butter in a separate bowl, add the sugar and beat until light and creamy. Add the egg yolks, one at a time, beating well after each addition, then stir in the melted chocolate. Add the ground almonds and beat in. Place the egg whites in a large, spotlessly clean, greasefree bowl and whisk until stiff but not dry. Stir 2 tablespoons of the whisked egg whites into the chocolate mixture, then carefully fold in the remainder.

3 Spoon the mixture into the prepared tin and bake in the oven for 35–40 minutes, or until well risen and just firm to the touch. Leave in the tin to cool completely. When cold, remove the cake from the tin and peel away the lining paper, then transfer to a serving plate. Spoon whipped cream over the top to decorate and dust with a little cinnamon. Serve, cut into slices.

mocha walnut meringue gâteau

serves 8   **prep: 25 mins, plus 1 hr cooling**   **cook: 1 hr 35 mins**

This deliciously crisp nutty meringue contrasts wonderfully with its creamy, brandy-laced filling, and is perfect for any occasion.

INGREDIENTS

4 egg whites

225 g/8 oz golden caster sugar

115 g/4 oz shelled walnuts, finely chopped

FILLING

175 g/6 oz plain chocolate

40 g/1½ oz unsalted butter

2 tbsp strong black coffee

2 tbsp brandy

175 ml/6 fl oz whipping cream

icing sugar, for dusting

variation

Instead of walnuts, add chopped toasted hazelnuts or ground almonds to the meringue.

cook's tip

Lining the baking sheets with non-stick baking paper makes it easier to remove the cooled meringues. Use a round-bladed knife to spread the meringues out on the baking sheets.

1 Preheat the oven to 140°C/275°F/Gas Mark 1. Line 2 baking sheets with non-stick baking paper. To make the meringue, place the egg whites in a large, clean, greasefree bowl and whisk until stiff but not dry. Whisk in half the sugar. Add the walnuts to the remaining sugar and mix together. Fold into the meringue mixture.

2 Spread the meringue into 2 x 20-cm/8-inch rounds on the baking sheets. Bake in the preheated oven for 1½ hours, or until completely dry. Leave in the oven to cool.

3 To make the filling, break the chocolate into pieces and place in a heatproof bowl with the butter, coffee and brandy. Set over a saucepan of gently simmering water until melted. Stir and leave to cool. Place the cream in a separate bowl and whip lightly, then stir in the chocolate mixture. Sandwich the meringue rounds together with the chocolate cream. Dust with sifted icing sugar before serving.

chocolate almond cake

serves 8
prep: 1 hr, plus 2 hrs ⏲
30 mins cooling/setting
cook: 40 mins ⏲

Chocolate and almonds complement each other perfectly in this delicious cake. Be warned though, one slice will never be enough!

INGREDIENTS

175 g/6 oz butter, plus extra
for greasing
175 g/6 oz plain chocolate
125 g/4½ oz caster sugar
4 eggs, separated
¼ tsp cream of tartar
6 tbsp self-raising flour
125 g/4½ oz ground almonds
1 tsp almond essence
125 g/4½ oz milk chocolate
2 tbsp butter
4 tbsp double cream
25 g/1 oz toasted flaked almonds
25 g/1 oz plain chocolate, to decorate

cook's tip

To toast almonds, place the almonds on a foil-lined grill rack and place under the preheated grill for 3–5 minutes, turning frequently. Take care as they burn very easily.

1 Preheat the oven to 190°C/375°F/Gas Mark 5. Grease and line the base of a 23-cm/9-inch round springform tin. Break the chocolate into pieces and put in a saucepan with the butter. Heat, stirring, until blended. Whisk 100 g/3½ oz of the sugar and egg yolks together until pale and creamy. Add the chocolate, beating until mixed.

2 Sift the cream of tartar and flour together and fold into the chocolate mixture with the ground almonds and almond essence.

3 Whisk the egg whites in a clean bowl until soft peaks form. Add the remaining caster sugar and whisk for 2 minutes, or until thick and glossy. Fold the egg whites into

the chocolate mixture and spoon into the tin. Bake in the hot oven for 40 minutes, or until just springy to the touch. Leave to cool.

4 Heat the milk chocolate, butter and cream together in a heatproof bowl set over a saucepan of gently simmering water. Remove from the heat and

beat for 2 minutes. Leave to cool for 30 minutes. Transfer the cake to a serving plate, spread the top with the chocolate mixture and sprinkle with the almonds. Melt the plain chocolate (see pages 9–10) and use to drizzle over the cake. Leave to set for 2 hours before serving.

chocolate lamington cake

cook: 45 mins   **prep: 25 mins, plus 1 hr 20 mins cooling/setting**   **serves 8**

This recipe is based on a famous Australian cake named after Lord Lamington, a former Governor of Queensland.

cook's tip

When piping cream, use a large star-shaped nozzle. Hold the piping bag in your hand and turn the top to come halfway down the sides of the bag. Fill and pull the sides of the bag up to the top.

INGREDIENTS

175 g/6 oz butter, plus extra for greasing

175 g/6 oz caster sugar

3 eggs, lightly beaten

150 g/5½ oz self-raising flour

2 tbsp cocoa powder

50 g/1¾ oz plain chocolate, broken into pieces

5 tbsp milk

1 tsp butter

125 g/4½ oz icing sugar

8 tbsp desiccated coconut

150 ml/5 fl oz double cream, whipped

1 Preheat the oven to 180°C/350°F/Gas Mark 4. Lightly grease a 450-g/1-lb loaf tin – preferably a long, thin tin measuring 7.5 x 25 cm/3 x 10 inches.

2 Beat the butter and sugar together in a bowl until light and fluffy. Gradually add the eggs, beating well after each addition. Sift the flour and cocoa powder together, then fold into the mixture.

3 Pour the mixture into the tin and smooth the top. Bake in the preheated oven for 40 minutes, or until springy to the touch. Cool in the tin for 5 minutes, then turn out on to a wire rack to cool completely.

4 Place the chocolate, milk and butter in a heatproof bowl and set over a saucepan of hot water. Stir until the chocolate has melted. Add the icing sugar and beat until smooth. Leave to cool until the icing is thick enough to spread, then spread it all over the cake. Sprinkle with the coconut and leave to set.

5 Cut a V-shaped wedge from the top of the cake. Place the cream in a piping bag fitted with a plain or star nozzle and pipe the cream down the centre of the gap left by the wedge. Replace the wedge of cake on top of the cream. Pipe another line of cream down either side of the wedge of cake, then serve.

almond & hazelnut gâteau

 cook: 25 mins   prep: 1 hr, plus 1 hr   serves 8
                      40 mins cooling/chilling

This is a light, nutty gâteau sandwiched together with chocolate cream. Simple to create, it is a cake you are sure to make again and again as it will be a winner with both family and friends.

variation

If you are making this gâteau for a special occasion, add 1 tablespoon of rum or brandy to the filling.

cook's tip

When dusting with icing sugar, use a small sieve or flour sifter to sift the sugar evenly over the top of the cake. This also prevents any lumps from falling on to the cake.

INGREDIENTS

butter, for greasing

4 eggs

100 g/3½ oz caster sugar

50 g/1¾ oz ground almonds

50 g/1¾ oz ground hazelnuts

5½ tbsp plain flour

50 g/1¾ oz flaked almonds

icing sugar, for dusting

FILLING

100 g/3½ oz plain chocolate

1 tbsp butter

300 ml/10 fl oz double cream

1 Preheat the oven to190°C/375°F/Gas Mark 5. Grease and line the bases of 2 x 18-cm/7-inch round sandwich tins.

2 Whisk the eggs and caster sugar together for 10 minutes, or until very light and foamy and the whisk leaves a trail that lasts a few seconds when lifted.

3 Fold in the ground almonds and hazelnuts, sift the flour and fold in with a metal spoon or spatula. Pour into the prepared tins.

4 Sprinkle the flaked almonds over the top of one of the cakes, then bake both cakes in the preheated oven for 15–20 minutes, or until springy to the touch.

5 Leave to cool in the tins for 5 minutes, then turn out on to wire racks to cool completely.

6 To make the filling, melt the chocolate (see pages 9–10), remove from the heat and stir in the butter. Cool. Whip the cream until holding its shape, then fold in the chocolate until mixed.

7 Place the cake without the extra almonds on a serving plate and spread the filling over it. Leave to set slightly, then place the almond-topped cake on top of the filling and leave to chill in the refrigerator for 1 hour. Dust with icing sugar and serve.

banana & chocolate teabread

serves 8   **prep: 10 mins, plus 40 mins cooling**   **cook: 50–60 mins**

This is a good cake to make when you have some overripe bananas in the fruit bowl. It is delicious served plain or buttered.

INGREDIENTS

115 g/4 oz butter, softened, plus extra for greasing

2 ripe bananas

85 g/3 oz golden caster sugar

2 eggs

200 g/7 oz self-raising flour

25 g/1 oz cocoa powder

1 tsp baking powder

1–2 tbsp milk

100 g/3½ oz plain chocolate chips

butter, to serve (optional)

variation

Add 55 g/2 oz chopped walnuts or the same amount of chopped dates to the mixture at the end of Step 2.

cook's tip

To make it slightly easier and quicker, you can mix the ingredients in a food processor, then stir in the chocolate chips by hand, if you like.

1 Preheat the oven to 180°C/350°F/Gas Mark 4. Grease and line a 900-g/2-lb loaf tin. Peel the bananas and place in a large bowl. Mash with a fork.

2 Add the butter, sugar and eggs, then sift the flour and cocoa and baking powders into the bowl. Beat

vigorously until smooth, adding enough milk to give a reluctant dropping consistency. Stir in the chocolate chips.

3 Spoon the mixture into the tin and bake in the preheated oven for 50–60 minutes, or until well risen and a skewer inserted in the centre comes out clean.

Leave in the tin for 5 minutes, then turn out on to a wire rack to cool completely. Serve sliced, with or without butter.

sicilian cassata

⏱ **cook: 30–40 mins**   🕐 **prep: 25 mins, plus 9 hrs cooling/chilling**   **serves 8**

This rich cake, with a filling of ricotta cheese, candied fruit, chopped nuts and plain chocolate, is a speciality of Sicily.

variation

If Marsala wine is unavailable, use dry sherry instead. Brandy would also work well in this cake.

cook's tip

If possible, buy pieces of candied peel and chop them yourself, rather than using ready-chopped peel. Store the cake in the refrigerator.

INGREDIENTS

175 g/6 oz butter, softened, plus extra for greasing

150 g/5½ oz self-raising flour

2 tbsp cocoa powder

1 tsp baking powder

175 g/6 oz golden caster sugar

3 eggs

icing sugar, for dusting

Chocolate Curls (see page 10), to decorate

FILLING

450 g/1 lb ricotta cheese

100 g/3½ oz plain chocolate, grated

115 g/4 oz golden caster sugar

3 tbsp Marsala wine

55 g/2 oz chopped candied peel

25 g/1 oz almonds, chopped

1 Preheat the oven to 190°C/375°F/Gas Mark 5. Grease and line the base of an 18-cm/7-inch round cake tin. Sift the flour and cocoa and baking powders into a large bowl. Add the butter, sugar and eggs and beat together thoroughly until smooth and creamy. Pour the mixture into the prepared tin and bake in the preheated oven for 30–40 minutes, or until well risen and firm to the touch. Leave in the tin for 5 minutes, then turn out on to a wire rack to cool completely.

2 Wash and dry the cake tin and grease and line it again. To make the filling, rub the ricotta through a sieve into a bowl. Add the grated chocolate, sugar and Marsala wine and beat together thoroughly until the mixture is light and fluffy. Stir in the candied peel and almonds.

3 Cut the thin crust off the top of the cake and discard. Cut the cake horizontally into 3 layers. Place the first slice in the prepared tin and cover with half the ricotta mixture. Repeat the layers, finishing with a cake layer. Press down lightly, cover with a plate and a weight and leave to chill in the refrigerator for 8 hours, or overnight. To serve, turn the cake out on to a serving plate. Dust with icing sugar and decorate with chocolate curls.

chocolate pear tart

serves 8

prep: 25 mins, plus
1 hr cooling/chilling

cook: 30 mins

The classic partnership of chocolate and pears appears in many forms, both hot and cold. This tart will soon become a favourite.

INGREDIENTS

115 g/4 oz plain flour, plus extra
for dusting

pinch of salt

2 tbsp caster sugar

115 g/4 oz unsalted butter, diced

1 egg yolk

1 tbsp lemon juice

115 g/4 oz plain chocolate, grated

4 pears

125 ml/4 fl oz single cream

1 egg, plus 1 egg yolk

½ tsp almond essence

3 tbsp caster sugar

1 fresh mint sprig, to decorate

cook's tip

Before baking, place the tart on a large baking sheet as the filling may leak out slightly during cooking. The tart is also easier to remove from the oven if placed on a baking sheet.

1 Sift the flour and the salt into a large bowl. Add the caster sugar and butter and mix well with a pastry blender or 2 forks until thoroughly incorporated. Stir in the egg yolk and lemon juice to form a dough. Form the dough into a ball, wrap in clingfilm and leave to chill in the refrigerator for 30 minutes.

2 Preheat the oven to 200°C/400°F/Gas Mark 6. Roll out the dough on a lightly floured work surface and use to line a 25-cm/ 10-inch loose-bottomed flan tin. Sprinkle the grated chocolate over the base of the pastry case. Peel the pears, cut them in half lengthways and remove the cores. Thinly slice

each pear half crossways and fan the slices out slightly. Using a spatula, scoop up each sliced pear half and arrange in the pastry case.

3 Beat the cream, egg, extra yolk and almond essence together and spoon over the pears. Sprinkle the sugar over the tart.

4 Bake in the preheated oven for 10 minutes. Reduce the oven temperature to 180°C/350°F/Gas Mark 4 and bake for a further 20 minutes, or until the pears are beginning to caramelize and the filling is just set. Remove from the oven and cool to room temperature before serving. Decorate with a fresh mint sprig and serve.

date & chocolate cake

cook: 40 mins   **prep: 25 mins, plus 20 mins cooling**   **serves: 6**

Moist and moreish, this fruity chocolate cake will prove to be a popular after-school snack.

variation

Replace the orange juice in the filling with the same quantity of lemon juice for a zestier flavour.

INGREDIENTS

115 g/4 oz unsalted butter
85 g/3 oz self-raising flour
115 g/4 oz dark chocolate pieces
1 tbsp grenadine
1 tbsp golden syrup
55 g/2 oz caster sugar
2 large eggs
2 tbsp ground rice
1 tbsp icing sugar, to decorate

FILLING
115 g/4 oz dried dates, chopped
1 tbsp orange juice
1 tbsp demerara sugar
25 g/1 oz blanched almonds, chopped
2 tbsp apricot jam

1   Grease and dust two 18-cm/7-inch sandwich tins with a little extra butter and flour. Place the broken pieces of chocolate, grenadine and syrup in the top of a double boiler or in a heatproof bowl set over a saucepan of barely simmering water. Stir over a low heat until the chocolate has melted and the mixture is smooth. Remove from the heat and leave to cool.

2   Cream the butter and caster sugar together until pale and fluffy. Gradually beat in the eggs and then the cooled chocolate mixture.

3   Sieve the flour into another bowl and stir in the ground rice. Fold the two mixtures together.

4   Divide the mixture between the prepared tins and smooth the surface. Bake in a preheated oven, 180°C/350°F/Gas Mark 4, for 20–25 minutes, until golden and firm to the touch. Turn out on to a wire rack to cool.

5   To make the filling, put all the ingredients into a saucepan and stir over a low heat for 4–5 minutes, until fully blended. Remove from the heat, leave to cool and then use the filling to sandwich the cakes together. Dust the top of the cake with icing sugar to decorate and serve.

lemon & chocolate tart

serves 8–10   **prep: 20 mins, plus ⏲ 30 mins chilling**   **cook: 1 hr 15 mins ⏲**

In this tart, a crisp chocolate pastry case is the perfect foil for the smooth, creamy lemon filling. It is the perfect end to a supper party.

INGREDIENTS

100 g/3½ oz plain flour

25 g/1 oz cocoa powder

75 g/2¾ oz butter

25 g/1 oz ground almonds

50 g/1¾ oz golden caster sugar

1 egg, beaten

Chocolate Curls (see page 10), to decorate

FILLING

4 eggs

1 egg yolk

200 g/7 oz golden caster sugar

150 ml/5 fl oz double cream

grated rind and juice of 2 lemons

variation

For an orange-flavoured tart, replace the grated rind and juice of 2 lemons with the grated rind and juice of 2 oranges.

cook's tip

Most lemons are waxed and sprayed before ending up in the supermarket, so if you are using grated lemon rind or zest in a cake or tart, try to buy unwaxed lemons.

1 Sift the flour and cocoa into a food processor. Add the butter, almonds, sugar and egg and process until the mixture forms a ball. Gather the dough together and press into a flattened ball. Place in the centre of a 22-cm/8½-inch loose-bottomed flan tin and press evenly over the bottom of the tin with your fingers, then work the pastry up the sides with your fingers and thumbs. Allow any excess pastry to go over the edge. Cover and chill for 30 minutes.

2 Preheat the oven to 200°C/400°F/Gas Mark 6. Trim off the excess pastry. Prick the pastry base lightly with a fork, then line with baking paper and fill with baking beans. Bake for 12–15 minutes, or until the pastry no longer looks raw. Remove the beans and paper, return to the oven and bake for 10 minutes, or until the pastry is firm. Leave to cool. Reduce the oven temperature to 150°C/300°F/Gas Mark 2.

3 To make the filling, whisk the whole eggs, egg yolk and sugar together until smooth. Add the cream and whisk again, then stir in the lemon rind and juice. Pour the filling into the pastry case and bake for 50 minutes, or until just set. When the tart is cooked, remove the flan ring and cool. Decorate with Chocolate Curls before serving.

chocolate fudge tart

cook: 1 hr 15 mins   **prep: 15 mins, plus 30 mins cooling**   **serves 6–8**

This rich, fudgy tart is sure to become a favourite, and is quick and easy to prepare using ready-made pastry. Serve with cream.

variation

For a special treat, replace the ready-made pastry with Rich Chocolate Pastry (see page 13).

cook's tip

The best way to transfer the rolled-out pastry to the tart tin is to roll the pastry gently on to the lightly floured rolling pin, lift it off the work surface and ease it into the tin.

INGREDIENTS

flour, for sprinkling
350 g/12 oz ready-made shortcrust pastry
icing sugar, for dusting

350 g/12 oz golden granulated sugar
100 g/3½ oz plain flour
½ tsp vanilla essence
6 eggs, beaten

FILLING
140 g/5 oz plain chocolate, finely chopped
175 g/6 oz butter, diced

TO DECORATE
150 ml/5 fl oz whipped cream
ground cinnamon

1 Preheat the oven to 200°C/400°F/Gas Mark 6. Roll out the pastry on a lightly floured work surface and use to line a 20-cm/8-inch deep loose-bottomed tart tin. Prick the pastry base lightly with a fork, then line with foil and fill with baking beans. Bake in the oven for 12–15 minutes, or until the pastry no longer looks raw.

Remove the beans and foil and bake for a further 10 minutes, or until the pastry is firm. Cool. Reduce the oven temperature to 180°C/350°F/Gas Mark 4.

2 To make the filling, place the chocolate and butter in a heatproof bowl and set over a saucepan of gently simmering water until melted. Stir until smooth, then remove from the heat and leave to cool. Place the sugar, flour, vanilla essence and eggs in a separate bowl and whisk until well blended. Stir in the butter and chocolate mixture.

3 Pour the filling into the pastry case and bake in the oven for 50 minutes, or until the filling is just set. Transfer to a wire rack to cool completely. Dust with icing sugar before serving with whipped cream sprinkled lightly with cinnamon.

pine kernel tartlets

serves 8   **prep: 40 mins, plus 1 hr ⟳ 40 mins cooling/chilling**   **cook: 45 mins ⟳**

Pine kernels and orange rind are very popular ingredients in Mediterranean dishes – here they add a twist of flavour to these tarts.

INGREDIENTS

1 quantity Extra-rich Shortcrust Pastry (see page 13)

plain flour, for dusting

55 g/2 oz good-quality plain chocolate

5 tbsp unsalted butter

175 g/6 oz plus 2 tbsp caster sugar

6 tbsp light brown sugar

6 tbsp milk

3½ tbsp golden syrup

finely grated rind of 2 large oranges and 2 tbsp freshly squeezed juice

1 tsp vanilla essence

3 large eggs, lightly beaten

100 g/3½ oz pine kernels

cook's tip

Cover the tartlets with a piece of baking paper for the last 5 minutes of the cooking time if the pastry is browning too much or beginning to burn.

1 Make the pastry (see page 13). Shape the dough into a ball, wrap in clingfilm and leave to chill in the refrigerator for 1 hour.

2 Preheat the oven to 200°C/400°F/Gas Mark 6. Roll the pastry out on a lightly floured work surface into 8 circles, each 15-cm/6-inch across. Use to line

8 loose-bottomed 10-cm/4-inch tartlet tins. Line each with baking paper to fit and fill with baking beans. Leave to chill in the refrigerator for 10 minutes.

3 Bake in the hot oven for 5 minutes. Remove the paper and beans and bake for 8 minutes. Cool on a wire rack. Reduce the temperature to 180°C/350°F/Gas Mark 4.

4 Meanwhile, break the chocolate into small pieces and place in a saucepan over a low heat. Add the butter and stir until blended.

5 Stir in the remaining ingredients. Place the tartlet cases on a baking tray and spoon the filling into the cases. Bake in the hot oven for 25–30 minutes, or until the

tops puff up and crack and feel set. Transfer to a wire rack and leave to cool for 15 minutes before unmoulding. Serve warm or at room temperature.

crispy chocolate pie

cook: 35–40 mins   **prep: 25 mins, plus 30 mins cooling**   **serves 6**

The whisky-flavoured chocolate filling makes this scrumptious pie very moreish. It is an excellent dessert for serving at a dinner party.

cook's tip

Replace the whisky with the same amount of brandy and replace the grated chocolate with Chocolate Curls (see page 10).

INGREDIENTS

2 tsp butter, for greasing

2 egg whites

115 g/4 oz ground almonds

25 g/1 oz ground rice

115 g/4 oz caster sugar

¼ tsp almond essence

225 g/8 oz plain chocolate

4 egg yolks

55 g/2 oz icing sugar

4 tbsp whisky

4 tbsp double cream

150 ml/5 fl oz whipped cream

55 g/2 oz plain chocolate, grated

1 Preheat the oven to 160°C/325°F/Gas Mark 3. Grease and line the base of a 20-cm/8-inch flan tin. Whisk the egg whites in a clean bowl until stiff peaks form. Fold in the ground almonds, ground rice, caster sugar and almond essence. Spread the mixture over the base and sides of the tin. Bake in the oven for 15 minutes.

2 Meanwhile, place the chocolate in the top of a double boiler or in a heatproof bowl set over a saucepan of barely simmering water and stir over a low heat until melted. Remove from the heat and leave to cool slightly, then beat in the egg yolks, icing sugar, whisky and the cream until thoroughly incorporated.

3 Remove the flan tin from the oven and pour in the chocolate mixture. Cover, return to the oven and bake for 20–25 minutes, or until set. Remove from the oven and cool completely.

4 Mix the whipped cream and 25 g/1 oz of the grated chocolate together in a bowl, then use to decorate the top of the pie. Top with the remaining grated chocolate, then serve immediately.

small cakes & pastries

Large cakes and gâteaux can look spectacular, but there is something about a pile of dainty 'finger' cakes or delicate pastries that shouts out, 'Eat me!' This selection of mouthwatering recipes includes light and fancy offerings for elegant tea parties, such as Chocolate Ginger Meringues (see page 180) or Raspberry & Chocolate Éclairs (see page 168), while for everyday occasions and family appeal you can't go wrong with Cup Cakes (see page 184), with white or plain chocolate varieties to choose from, or Chocolate Chip Brownies, with or without the Fudge Sauce (see page 160), which are easy to make and are sure to disappear almost the moment you have finished making them.

Why not start the day with a little indulgence in the form of Pains au Chocolat (see page 176), warm and inviting from the oven, Pecan & Chocolate Pancakes (see page 169) or Double Chocolate Chunk Muffins (see page 162) – perfect for a weekend brunch? Many of these individual cakes and pastries also make wonderful desserts, served warm or cold. So bring your evening meal and day to a close in style with White Chocolate Tarts (see page 166) or Pistachio & Chocolate Filo Fingers (see page 174), served with freshly brewed coffee.

mocha brownies with soured cream icing

**makes 9 large or
16 small brownies**

**prep: 20 mins, plus
30 mins cooling**

cook: 30 mins

*A hint of coffee and soured cream in the topping give these
brownies a more sophisticated flavour.*

INGREDIENTS

55 g/2 oz butter, plus extra
for greasing

115 g/4 oz plain chocolate,
broken into pieces

175 g/6 oz dark muscovado sugar

2 eggs

2 tbsp strong coffee, cooled

85 g/3 oz plain flour

½ tsp baking powder

pinch of salt

55 g/2 oz shelled walnuts, chopped

ICING

115 g/4 oz plain chocolate,
broken into pieces

150 ml/5 fl oz soured cream

variation

These brownies can be made without
the icing and served warm with vanilla
ice cream or whipped cream.

cook's tip

Do not leave the brownies to set in the
refrigerator but place them in the cake
tin in a cool place. Store any un-iced
brownies in an airtight container for
up to 3 days.

1 Preheat the oven
to 180°C/350°F/Gas
Mark 4. Grease a 20-cm/8-inch
square cake tin with butter
and line with baking paper.
Place the chocolate and butter
in a small heatproof bowl and
set over a saucepan of gently
simmering water until melted.
Stir until smooth. Remove from
the heat and leave to cool.

2 Beat the sugar and eggs
together until pale and
thick. Fold in the chocolate
mixture and coffee. Mix well.
Sift the flour, baking powder
and salt into the mixture and
fold in. Fold in the walnuts.
Pour the mixture into the tin
and bake in the oven for
20–25 minutes, or until set.
Leave in the tin to cool.

3 To make the icing,
melt the chocolate (see
pages 9–10). Stir in the soured
cream and beat until evenly
blended. Spoon the topping
over the brownies and make a
swirling pattern with a palette
knife. Leave in a cool place to
set. Cut into squares, then
remove from the tin and serve.

chocolate chip brownies with fudge sauce

cook: 55–60 mins　　　**prep: 25 mins**　　　**makes 9 large or 16 small brownies**

Plain chocolate, cocoa and white chocolate chips make these brownies a chocolate-lover's dream, and when served with a chocolate fudge sauce, they are stunning!

variation

The brownies can be left to cool completely and served as cakes without the fudge sauce.

cook's tip

To make a more richly flavoured chocolate fudge sauce, use the same amount of light or dark muscovado sugar instead of golden caster sugar.

INGREDIENTS

115 g/4 oz butter, plus extra for greasing

115 g/4 oz plain chocolate, broken into pieces

300 g/10½ oz golden caster sugar

pinch of salt

1 tsp vanilla essence

2 large eggs

115 g/4 oz plain flour

2 tbsp cocoa powder

100 g/3½ oz white chocolate chips

FUDGE SAUCE

55 g/2 oz butter

225 g/8 oz golden caster sugar

150 ml/5 fl oz milk

250 ml/9 fl oz double cream

150 ml/5 fl oz golden syrup

200 g/7 oz plain chocolate, broken into pieces

1 Preheat the oven to 180°C/350°F/Gas Mark 4. Grease and line the base of an 18-cm/7-inch square cake tin. Place the butter and chocolate in a heatproof bowl and set over a saucepan of simmering water until melted. Stir until smooth. Leave to cool slightly. Stir in the sugar, salt and vanilla essence. Add the eggs, one at a time, stirring well each time, until blended.

2 Sift the flour and cocoa powder into the mixture and beat until smooth. Stir in the chocolate chips, then pour the mixture into the tin. Bake in the oven for 35–40 minutes, or until the top is evenly coloured and a cocktail stick inserted into the centre comes out almost clean. Leave to cool slightly.

3 To make the sauce, place the butter, sugar, milk, cream and syrup in a small saucepan and heat gently until the sugar has dissolved. Bring to the boil and stir for 10 minutes, or until the mixture is caramel coloured. Remove from the heat and add the chocolate. Stir until smooth. Cut the brownies into squares and serve with the sauce.

double chocolate chunk muffins

makes 12 **prep: 15 mins, plus** ⏲ **40 mins cooling/setting** **cook: 20 mins** ⏲

Muffins are very easy to make, as all the ingredients are mixed quickly together and then poured into the paper cases.

INGREDIENTS

200 g/7 oz plain flour

25 g/1 oz cocoa powder, plus extra for dusting

1 tbsp baking powder

1 tsp ground cinnamon

115 g/4 oz golden caster sugar

185 g/6½ oz white chocolate, broken into pieces

2 eggs

100 ml/3½ fl oz sunflower oil

225 ml/8 fl oz milk

variation

Instead of white chocolate, use plain or milk chocolate to spread on top of the muffins and dust with a little ground cinnamon, if you like.

cook's tip

When stirring the muffin mixture together, do not overstir or the muffins will be tough. The muffin mixture should be quite lumpy.

1 Preheat the oven to 200°C/400°F/Gas Mark 6. Line a 12-hole muffin tin with double muffin paper cases. Sift the flour, cocoa and baking powders and cinnamon into a large bowl. Stir in the sugar and 125 g/4½ oz of the white chocolate.

2 Place the eggs and oil in a separate bowl and whisk until frothy, then gradually whisk in the milk. Stir into the dry ingredients until just blended. Spoon the mixture into the paper cases, filling each three-quarters full. Bake in the preheated oven for 20 minutes, or until well risen and springy to the touch. Leave to cool for 2 minutes, then remove the muffins and cool on a wire rack.

3 Melt the remaining white chocolate (see pages 9–10) and spread over the muffins. Leave to set, then dust the tops with a little cocoa powder and serve.

fudge nut muffins

⏲ **cook: 25–30 mins**   ⏱ **prep: 10 mins, plus 30 mins cooling**   **makes 12**

Chewy pieces of fudge give these muffins a lovely texture and contrast with the crunchiness of the nuts.

variation

To make these muffins really chocolatey, replace the vanilla fudge with milk or plain chocolate fudge, if you like.

INGREDIENTS

250 g/9 oz plain flour

4 tsp baking powder

85 g/3 oz golden caster sugar

6 tbsp crunchy peanut butter

1 egg, beaten

60 g/2¼ oz butter, melted

175 ml/6 fl oz milk

150 g/5½ oz vanilla fudge, cut into small pieces

3 tbsp roughly chopped unsalted peanuts

1 Preheat the oven to 200°C/400°F/Gas Mark 6. Line a 12-hole muffin tin with double muffin paper cases. Sift the flour and baking powder into a bowl. Stir in the sugar. Add the peanut butter and stir until the mixture resembles breadcrumbs.

2 Place the egg, butter and milk in a separate bowl and beat together until blended, then stir into the dry ingredients until just blended. Lightly stir in the fudge pieces. Spoon the mixture into the muffin cases.

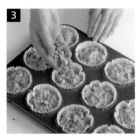

3 Sprinkle the chopped peanuts on top and bake in the preheated oven for 20–25 minutes, or until well risen and firm to the touch. Leave to cool for 2 minutes, then remove the muffins to a wire rack to cool completely before serving.

chocolate butterfly cakes

serves 12   **prep: 15 mins, plus 30 mins cooling**   **cook: 15 mins**

Filled with a tangy lemon buttercream, these appealing cakes will be a favourite with adults and children alike.

INGREDIENTS

125 g/4½ oz soft margarine

125 g/4½ oz caster sugar

150 g/5½ oz self-raising flour

2 large eggs

2 tbsp cocoa powder

25 g/1 oz plain chocolate, melted

icing sugar, for dusting

BUTTERCREAM

100 g/3½ oz unsalted butter, softened

225 g/8 oz icing sugar, sifted

grated rind of ½ lemon

1 tbsp lemon juice

variation

For a chocolate buttercream, beat the butter and icing sugar together, then beat in 25 g/1 oz melted plain chocolate.

1 Preheat the oven to 180°C/350°F/Gas Mark 4. Place 12 paper cake cases in a bun tray. Place all of the ingredients for the cakes, except for the melted chocolate, in a large bowl and, using an electric whisk, mix until the mixture is just smooth. Mix in the chocolate.

2 Spoon equal amounts of the cake mixture into each paper case, filling them three-quarters full. Bake in the oven for 15 minutes, or until springy to the touch. Transfer the cakes to a wire rack and leave to cool completely.

3 Meanwhile, make the buttercream. Place the butter in a large bowl and beat until fluffy, then gradually beat in the icing sugar. Beat in the lemon rind and gradually add the lemon juice, beating well.

4 When cold, cut the top off each cake, using a serrated knife. Cut each cake top in half.

5 Spread or pipe the buttercream over the cut surface of each cake and push the 2 cut pieces of cake top into the buttercream to form wings. Sprinkle the cakes with icing sugar and serve.

white chocolate tarts

⏱ **cook: 20 mins**   ⏲ **prep: 40 mins, plus 1 hr 35 mins chilling**   **makes 12**

These dainty little tarts are wonderful for serving after dinner with coffee instead of chocolates, or even as a delicious afternoon treat.

variation

For a touch of decadence, use Basic Chocolate Pastry (see page 13). You could also replace the white chocolate in the filling with plain.

cook's tip

When buying vanilla pods, choose pods that are shiny, pliable and sticky. The seeds have a stronger flavour than the pod. Store a pod in a jar of caster sugar to flavour the sugar.

INGREDIENTS

225 g/8 oz plain flour, plus extra for dusting

25 g/1 oz golden caster sugar

150 g/5½ oz chilled butter, diced

2 egg yolks

2 tbsp cold water

plain Chocolate Curls (see page 10), to decorate

cocoa powder, for dusting

FILLING

1 vanilla pod

400 ml/14 fl oz double cream

350 g/12 oz white chocolate, broken into pieces

1 Place the flour and sugar in a bowl. Add the butter and rub it in until the mixture resembles fine breadcrumbs. Place the egg yolks and water in a separate bowl and mix together. Stir into the dry ingredients and mix to form a dough. Knead for 1 minute, or until smooth. Wrap in clingfilm and chill in the refrigerator for 20 minutes.

2 Preheat the oven to 200°C/400°F/Gas Mark 6. Roll out the pastry on a floured work surface and use to line 12 tartlet moulds. Prick the bases, cover and chill in the refrigerator for 15 minutes. Line the cases with foil and baking beans and bake for 10 minutes. Remove the beans and foil and cook for a further 5 minutes. Leave to cool.

3 To make the filling, split the vanilla pod lengthways and scrape out the black seeds with a knife. Place the seeds in a saucepan with the cream and heat until almost boiling. Place the chocolate in a heatproof bowl and pour over the hot cream. Keep stirring until smooth. Whisk the mixture with an electric whisk until thickened and the whisk leaves a trail when lifted. Chill in the refrigerator for 30 minutes, then whisk until soft peaks form. Divide the filling between the pastry cases and chill for 30 minutes. Decorate with Chocolate Curls and dust with cocoa powder.

raspberry & chocolate éclairs

makes 20–24

prep: 20 mins, plus 25 mins cooling/setting

cook: 40 mins

These small éclairs are perfect for serving at a summer tea party.
They look particularly appealing arranged on a pretty serving plate.

INGREDIENTS
55 g/2 oz butter
150 ml/5 fl oz water
70 g/2½ oz plain flour, sifted
2 eggs, beaten

FILLING AND TOPPING
175 ml/6 fl oz double cream
1 tbsp icing sugar
175 g/6 oz fresh raspberries
85 g/3 oz plain chocolate, broken into pieces

variation

Instead of piping the choux mixture, you can simply spoon it on to the dampened baking sheets.

cook's tip

The raw piped choux mixture can be made a few days ahead and frozen, then baked directly from the freezer for 5 minutes longer than usual.

1 Preheat the oven to 220°C/425°F/Gas Mark 7. To make the pastry, place the butter and water in a heavy-based saucepan and bring to the boil over a low heat. Add the flour, all at once, and beat thoroughly until the mixture leaves the side of the saucepan. Leave to cool slightly, then vigorously beat in the eggs, a little at a time.

2 Spoon the mixture into a piping bag fitted with a 1-cm/½-inch nozzle and pipe 20–24 x 7.5-cm/3-inch lengths on to dampened baking sheets. Bake in the preheated oven for 10 minutes, then reduce the oven temperature to 190°C/375°F/Gas Mark 5 and bake for a further 20 minutes, or until crisp and golden brown. Split the side of each éclair to let the steam escape, and transfer to a wire rack to cool completely.

3 To make the filling, place the cream and icing sugar in a bowl and whip until thick. Spoon into the éclairs. Place a few raspberries in each éclair. To make the topping, melt the chocolate (see pages 9–10) and spread a little on top of each éclair. Leave to set, then transfer to a large serving plate and serve.

pains au chocolat

cook: 15–20 mins

prep: 40 mins, plus 7 hrs rising/chilling

makes 8

There is nothing more irresistible than the sight and smell of freshly baked pains au chocolat emerging from the oven.

variation

Replace the plain chocolate with the same quantity of milk chocolate, or use milk chocolate chips.

cook's tip

If you are making the pains au chocolat for breakfast, prepare them the night before, cover and refrigerate overnight. Leave at room temperature for 30 minutes before baking.

INGREDIENTS

100 g/3½ oz butter, plus extra for greasing

250 g/9 oz strong white bread flour, plus extra for dusting

1 tsp salt

2 tsp easy-blend dried yeast

175 ml/6 fl oz milk

25 g/1 oz golden caster sugar

1 tbsp oil, plus extra for brushing

115 g/4 oz plain chocolate, roughly chopped

GLAZE

1 egg yolk

2 tbsp milk

 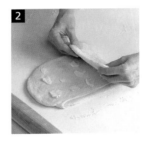 

1 Grease a baking sheet. Sift the flour and salt into a bowl and stir in the yeast. Make a well in the centre. Heat the milk in a pan until tepid. Add the sugar and oil and stir until the sugar has dissolved. Stir into the flour and mix well. Turn the dough out on to a lightly floured work surface and knead until smooth, then place in an oiled bowl. Cover and leave to rise in a warm place for 2–3 hours, or until doubled in size.

2 Knead on a floured work surface and roll into a rectangle 3 times as long as it is wide. Divide the butter into thirds. Dot one portion over the top two-thirds of the dough, leaving a 1-cm/ ½-inch margin around the edges. Fold the lower third up and the top third down. Seal the edges. Give the dough a half-turn. Roll into a rectangle. Repeat the process twice, then fold in half. Place in an oiled polythene bag. Chill for 1 hour.

3 Preheat the oven to 220°C/425°F/Gas Mark 7. Cut the dough in half and roll out into 2 rectangles of 30 x 15 cm/12 x 6 inches. Cut each half into 4 rectangles of 15 x 7.5 cm/6 x 3 inches. Sprinkle chocolate along one short end of each and roll up. Place on the baking sheet in a warm place for 2–3 hours, or until doubled in size. To glaze, mix the egg yolk and milk and brush over the rolls. Bake for 15–20 minutes, or until golden and well risen.

chocolate coconut squares

makes 9   **prep: 15 mins, plus** ⟳ **1 hr cooling/setting**   **cook: 35 mins** ⟳

These biscuits consist of a chewy coconut layer resting on a crisp chocolate biscuit base, cut into squares to serve.

INGREDIENTS

6 tbsp butter or margarine, plus extra for greasing

225 g/8 oz plain chocolate digestive biscuits

175 g/6 oz canned evaporated milk

1 egg, beaten

1 tsp vanilla essence

2 tbsp caster sugar

6 tbsp self-raising flour, sifted

125 g/4½ oz desiccated coconut

50 g/1¾ oz plain chocolate (optional)

variation

Add 25 g/1 oz melted white chocolate to the mixture in Step 3. Alternatively, colour the mixture pink with 1 teaspoon of red food colouring.

cook's tip

Store the coconut squares in an airtight container for up to 4 days. They can be frozen, undecorated for up to 2 months. Thaw at room temperature before eating.

1 Preheat the oven to 190°C/375°F/Gas Mark 5. Grease and line the base of a shallow 20-cm/8-inch square cake tin. Place the biscuits in a polythene bag and crush with a rolling pin. Alternatively, place them in a food processor and process until crushed.

2 Melt the butter or margarine in a saucepan and stir in the crushed biscuits until well blended. Press the mixture into the base of the cake tin.

3 Beat the evaporated milk, egg, vanilla essence and sugar together until smooth. Stir in the flour

and desiccated coconut. Pour the mixture over the biscuit base and smooth the top. Bake in the preheated oven for 30 minutes, or until the coconut topping is firm and just golden.

4 Leave to cool in the cake tin for 5 minutes, then cut into 9 squares. Leave to cool completely in the tin.

Carefully remove the squares from the tin and place them on a board. Melt the plain chocolate (see pages 9–10) and drizzle it over the squares to decorate them. Leave the chocolate to set before serving.

chocolate ginger meringues

makes 8

prep: 15 mins, plus ⏲ 1 hr setting

cook: 1 hr 35 mins ⏲

These meringues are flecked with chocolate and sandwiched with a delicious ginger-flavoured cream.

INGREDIENTS

225 g/8 oz plain chocolate

4 egg whites

225 g/8 oz golden caster sugar

FILLING

300 ml/10 fl oz double cream

3 pieces stem ginger, finely chopped, plus 1 tbsp ginger syrup from the jar

cook's tip

Take care not to overwhisk the meringue mixture. Add the sugar a little at a time, whisking after each addition, then whisk in the grated chocolate with care.

1 Preheat the oven to 120°C/250°F/Gas Mark ½. Line 2 baking sheets with non-stick baking paper. Grate half the chocolate. Place the egg whites in a large, clean, greasefree bowl and whisk until stiff but not dry. Whisk in half the sugar, a little at a time. Mix the grated chocolate with the remaining sugar. Fold into the mixture.

2 Pipe or spoon 16 tablespoonfuls of the meringue mixture on to the prepared baking sheets. Bake in the preheated oven for 1½ hours, or until dry. Transfer to wire racks to cool. Melt the remaining chocolate (see pages 9–10) and spread a little over the base of each meringue. Leave the meringues on wire racks to set.

3 To make the filling, place the cream in a bowl and whip until thick. Stir in the chopped ginger and ginger syrup. Sandwich the meringues together in pairs with the ginger cream before serving.

banana & chocolate triangles

cook: 14–16 mins   prep: 15 mins   makes 12

These crisp little parcels can be served as a tasty party snack,
or with coffee at the end of a meal.

variation

For an extra special chocolate sauce,
add 1 tablespoon of brandy to the
cream and chocolate in the saucepan
in Step 3. Proceed as in main recipe.

INGREDIENTS

1 banana

25 g/1 oz plain chocolate chips

4 sheets of filo pastry, measuring

18 x 30 cm/7 x 12 inches

55 g/2 oz butter, melted

SAUCE

150 ml/5 fl oz single cream

55 g/2 oz plain chocolate,

broken into pieces

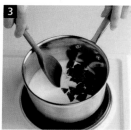

1 Preheat the oven
to 180°C/350°F/Gas
Mark 4. Peel the banana, place
in a bowl and mash with a
fork. Stir in the chocolate
chips. Cover the filo sheets
with a tea towel to prevent
them drying out. Brush a filo
rectangle with melted butter
and cut lengthways into
3 strips, 6 cm/2½ inches wide.

2 Spoon a little of the
banana mixture on to
the bottom end of each strip,
then fold the corner of the
pastry over to enclose it in a
triangle. Continue folding along
the whole length of the strip to
make a triangular parcel. Place
on a large baking sheet with
the seam underneath. Repeat
with the remaining pastry and

filling. Bake in the preheated
oven for 10–12 minutes, or
until golden brown.

3 To make the sauce,
place the cream and
chocolate in a saucepan and
heat gently until the chocolate
has melted. Stir until smooth.
Serve the pastries immediately
with the sauce.

chocolate hazelnut palmiers

⏱ **cook: 10–15 mins**   ⏱ **prep: 5 mins, plus 30 mins cooling**   **makes 26**

These delicious chocolate and hazelnut biscuits are very simple to make, and they are ideal for birthday parties. For very young children, leave out the chopped nuts.

variation

For an extra chocolate flavour, dip the palmiers in melted plain chocolate to half-cover each biscuit.

cook's tip

When rolling out pastry on the work surface, only use a small amount of flour as too much flour will affect the consistency of the pastry.

INGREDIENTS

butter, for greasing

375 g/13 oz ready-made puff pastry

plain flour, for dusting

8 tbsp chocolate hazelnut spread

50 g/1¾ oz chopped toasted hazelnuts

2 tbsp caster sugar

1 Preheat the oven to 220°C/425°F/Gas Mark 7. Lightly grease a baking tray. Roll out the pastry on a floured work surface to a rectangle measuring 38 x 23 cm/15 x 9 inches.

2 Using a palette knife, spread the chocolate spread over the pastry. Sprinkle the hazelnuts over the top.

3 Roll up one long side of the pastry to the centre, then roll up the other side so that they meet in the centre. Where the pieces meet, dampen the edges with water to join them. Using a sharp knife, cut into thin slices. Place each slice on to the prepared baking tray and flatten slightly with a palette knife. Sprinkle the slices with the caster sugar.

4 Bake in the preheated oven for 10–15 minutes, or until golden. Transfer to a wire rack to cool, then serve.

cup cakes

makes about 20

**prep: 20 mins, plus ⟳
1 hr cooling/setting**

cook: 35 mins ⟳

*These tasty little cakes are light and moist with a tempting fudgy
chocolate topping. Perfect for serving at any time of the day.*

INGREDIENTS

200 ml/7 fl oz water

85 g/3 oz butter

85 g/3 oz golden caster sugar

1 tbsp golden syrup

3 tbsp milk

1 tsp vanilla essence

1 tsp bicarbonate of soda

2 tbsp cocoa powder

225 g/8 oz plain flour

ICING

50 g/1¾ oz plain chocolate,
broken into pieces

4 tbsp water

50 g/1¾ oz butter

50 g/1¾ oz white chocolate,
broken into pieces

350 g/12 oz icing sugar

TO DECORATE

crystallized rose petals

crystallized violets

variation

Instead of the crystallized flower
petals, the cakes could be decorated
with Chocolate Curls (see page 10)
or chopped hazelnuts.

cook's tip

It is worthwhile investing in a set of
cook's measuring spoons. Accuracy is
particularly important when measuring
bicarbonate of soda.

1 Preheat the oven
to 180°C/350°F/Gas
Mark 4. Place paper bun cases
in 2 bun tins. Place the water,
butter, sugar and syrup in a
saucepan. Heat gently, stirring,
until the sugar has dissolved,
then bring to the boil. Reduce
the heat and cook gently for
5 minutes. Remove from the
heat and leave to cool. Place
the milk and vanilla essence in

a bowl. Add the bicarbonate of
soda and stir to dissolve. Sift
the cocoa powder and flour
into a separate bowl and add
the syrup mixture. Stir in the
milk and beat until smooth.

2 Carefully spoon the
mixture into the paper
cases to within two-thirds of
the tops. Bake in the oven for
20 minutes, or until well risen

and firm to the touch. Leave to
cool on a wire rack. To make
the icing, place the plain
chocolate in a small heatproof
bowl with half the water and
half the butter and set the
bowl over a saucepan of gently
simmering water until melted.
Stir until smooth and leave
over the water. Repeat with
the white chocolate and
remaining water and butter.

3 Stir half the icing sugar
into each bowl and beat
until smooth and fudgy. Divide
the icings between the cakes,
filling to the top of the paper
cases. Leave to cool, then place
a crystallized rose petal on each
of the plain chocolate iced
cakes and a crystallized violet
on each white chocolate iced
cake. Leave the icing to set
before serving.

apricot & chocolate chip cookies

cook: 13–15 mins   prep: 20 mins, plus 30 mins cooling   makes 12–14

The apricots in these deliciously moist cookies give them a lovely fruity flavour. If there are any left, store in an airtight container.

variation

As an alternative to dried apricots, try other dried fruit, such as dried cranberries, cherries or raisins.

cook's tip

When baking, it is important to preheat the oven before the cookies and cakes are baked, otherwise they will not cook properly.

INGREDIENTS

85 g/3 oz butter, softened, plus extra for greasing

25 g/1 oz golden granulated sugar

55 g/2 oz light muscovado sugar

½ tsp vanilla essence

1 egg

175 g/6 oz self-raising flour

115 g/4 oz plain chocolate, roughly chopped

115 g/4 oz no-soak dried apricots, roughly chopped

1 Preheat the oven to 180°C/350°F/Gas Mark 4. Grease 2 baking sheets. Place the butter, granulated sugar, muscovado sugar and vanilla essence in a bowl and beat together. Gradually beat in the egg until light and fluffy.

2 Sift the flour over the mixture and fold in, then fold in the chocolate and apricots.

3 Drop tablespoonfuls of the mixture on to the prepared baking sheets, allowing space for the cookies to spread. Bake in the preheated oven for 13–15 minutes, or until crisp outside but still soft inside. Leave to cool on the baking sheets for 2 minutes, then transfer to wire racks to cool completely.

chocolate chip oaties

makes about 20

prep: 15 mins, plus 30 mins cooling

cook: 15 mins

Porridge oats give a light texture and a nutty flavour to these cookies. They are superb if served with a cup of fresh coffee.

INGREDIENTS

115 g/4 oz butter, softened, plus extra for greasing

115 g/4 oz light muscovado sugar

1 egg

100 g/3½ oz porridge oats

1 tbsp milk

1 tsp vanilla essence

125 g/4½ oz plain flour

1 tbsp cocoa powder

½ tsp baking powder

175 g/6 oz plain chocolate, broken into pieces

175 g/6 oz milk chocolate, broken into pieces

variation

Replace the plain and milk chocolate with 175 g/6 oz milk chocolate chips and 175 g/6 oz chopped pecan nuts.

cook's tip

After baking, biscuits and cookies must be left on the baking sheet for 2 minutes as this ensures they do not fall apart when transferred to a wire rack to cool.

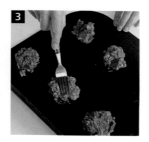

1 Preheat the oven to 180°C/350°F/Gas Mark 4. Grease 2 baking sheets. Place the butter and sugar in a bowl and beat together until light and fluffy.

2 Beat in the egg, then add the oats, milk and vanilla essence. Beat together until well blended. Sift the flour and cocoa and baking powders into the mixture and stir. Stir in the chocolate pieces.

3 Place dessertspoonfuls of the mixture on the prepared baking sheets and flatten slightly with a fork. Bake in the preheated oven for 15 minutes, or until slightly risen and firm. Cool on the baking sheets for 2 minutes, then transfer to wire racks to cool completely.

double chocolate chip cookies

makes about 24

prep: 15 mins, plus 20 mins cooling

cook: 10–12 mins

Boasting both white and dark chocolate chips, these cookies are the ultimate treat for chocolate-lovers.

INGREDIENTS

200 g/7 oz butter, softened, plus extra for greasing

200 g/7 oz golden caster sugar

½ tsp vanilla essence

1 large egg

225 g/8 oz plain flour

pinch of salt

1 tsp bicarbonate of soda

115 g/4 oz white chocolate chips

115 g/4 oz plain chocolate chips

cook's tip

If you prefer a crisp cookie, rather than soft inside, cook them for a little bit longer, about 13–15 minutes, then proceed as in main recipe.

1 Preheat the oven to 180°C/350°F/Gas Mark 4. Grease 2 baking sheets with butter. Place the butter, sugar and vanilla essence in a large bowl and beat together. Gradually beat in the egg until the mixture is light and fluffy.

2 Sift the flour, salt and bicarbonate of soda over the mixture and fold in. Fold in the chocolate chips.

3 Drop dessertspoonfuls of the mixture on to the prepared baking sheets, allowing room for expansion during cooking. Bake in the hot oven for 10–12 minutes, or until crisp outside but still soft inside. Leave to cool on the baking sheets for 2 minutes, then transfer to wire racks to cool completely.

white chocolate cookies

⏱ **cook: 10–12 mins**   🕐 **prep: 15 mins, plus   makes 24**
                                       30 mins cooling

*These chunky cookies melt in the mouth and the white
chocolate gives them a deliciously rich flavour.*

variation
Replace the white chocolate with the same amount of plain or milk chocolate, if you prefer.

INGREDIENTS

125 g/4½ oz butter, softened, plus extra

for greasing

125 g/4½ oz soft brown sugar

1 egg, beaten

200 g/7 oz self-raising flour

pinch of salt

125 g/4½ oz white chocolate,

roughly chopped

50 g/1¾ oz Brazil nuts, chopped

1 Preheat the oven to 190°C/375°F/Gas Mark 5. Lightly grease several baking trays, enough to accommodate 24 cookies. Cream the butter and sugar together in a large bowl until light and fluffy. Gradually add the beaten egg to the creamed mixture, beating well after each addition.

2 Sift the flour and salt into the creamed mixture and blend well. Stir in the white chocolate chunks and the chopped Brazil nuts.

3 Drop heaped teaspoons of the mixture on to the baking trays. Do not put more than 6 teaspoons of the mixture on to each tray as they will spread during cooking.

4 Bake in the preheated oven, for 10–12 minutes, or until just golden brown. Transfer the cookies to wire racks and leave until completely cold before serving.

chocolate pretzels

cook: 20 mins   **prep: 30 mins, plus 1 hr 15 mins chilling/setting**   **makes 30**

If you thought of pretzels as savouries, then think again. These are fun to make and prove that pretzels come in a sweet variety, too.

---

variation

For a change, dip the whole pretzel in the melted chocolate and sprinkle the tops with chopped nuts.

---

cook's tip

The pretzels can be stored in an airtight container for up to 3 days. Make sure the pretzels are not too close together in the container, otherwise they may stick to each other.

INGREDIENTS

100 g/3½ oz unsalted butter, plus extra for greasing

100 g/3½ oz caster sugar

1 egg

225 g/8 oz plain flour

2 tbsp cocoa powder

TO FINISH

1 tbsp butter

100 g/3½ oz plain chocolate

icing sugar, for dusting

1 Lightly grease a baking tray. Beat the butter and sugar together in a large bowl until light and fluffy. Beat in the egg. Sift the flour and cocoa powder together and gradually beat in to form a soft dough. Use your fingers to incorporate the last of the flour and bring the dough together. Chill in the refrigerator for 15 minutes.

2 Preheat the oven to 190°C/375°F/Gas Mark 5. Break pieces from the dough and roll into sausage shapes 10-cm/4-inches long and 5-mm/¼-inch thick. Twist into pretzel shapes by making a circle, then twist the ends through each other to form a letter 'B'. Place on the baking tray, allowing room for expansion during cooking.

3 Bake in the hot oven for 8–12 minutes. Leave to cool slightly on the baking tray, then transfer to a wire rack to cool completely.

4 Melt the butter and chocolate in a bowl set over a saucepan of gently simmering water, stirring to blend. Dip half of each pretzel into the chocolate and allow the excess chocolate to drip back into the bowl. Place the pretzels on a sheet of baking paper and leave to set. When set, dust the non-chocolate coated side of each pretzel with icing sugar before serving.

chocolate wheatmeals

makes 20　　**prep: 10 mins, plus** 🕑 **50 mins cooling/setting**　　**cook: 25 mins** 🕑

A good everyday biscuit, these wheatmeals will keep well in an airtight container for at least 1 week. Dip in white, milk or plain chocolate and serve as a tasty mid-morning snack

INGREDIENTS

6 tbsp butter, plus extra for greasing

100 g/3½ oz demerara sugar

1 egg

25 g/1 oz wheatgerm

125 g/4½ oz wholemeal self-raising flour

6 tbsp self raising flour, sifted

125 g/4½ oz chocolate

variation

If you like, add 55 g/2 oz chopped mixed nuts to the mixture in Step 1 and proceed as in main recipe.

cook's tip

These biscuits can be frozen very successfully. Freeze them at the end of Step 3 for up to 3 months. Thaw and then dip them in melted chocolate.

1 Preheat the oven to 180°C/350°F/Gas Mark 4. Grease a baking tray. Beat the butter and sugar until fluffy. Add the egg and beat well. Stir in the wheatgerm and flours. Bring the mixture together with your hands.

2 Roll rounded teaspoons of the mixture into balls and place on the prepared baking tray, allowing room for expansion during cooking.

3 Flatten the biscuits slightly with a fork, then bake in the preheated oven for 15–20 minutes, or until golden. Leave to cool on the baking tray for a few minutes before transferring to a wire rack to cool completely.

4 Melt the chocolate (see pages 9–10), then dip each biscuit in the chocolate to cover the bases and come a little way up the sides. Leave the excess chocolate to drip back into the bowl. Place the biscuits on a sheet of baking paper and leave to set in a cool place before serving.

chocolate orange biscuits

⏲ **cook: 10–12 mins**　　　🕐 **prep: 15 mins, plus**　　　**makes 30**
　　　　　　　　　　　　　　50 mins cooling/setting

These delicious chocolate biscuits have a tangy orange icing.
Children love them, especially if different shaped cutters are used.

variation

You can also make chocolate lemon biscuits. Replace the orange juice with the same amount of lemon juice.

cook's tip

You can buy a variety of biscuit cutters from kitchen shops. They are sold individually or as sets and are available in different sizes and shapes. For this recipe use a fluted round cutter.

INGREDIENTS

6 tbsp butter, softened

6 tbsp caster sugar

1 egg

1 tbsp milk

225 g/8 oz plain flour, plus

extra for dusting

2 tbsp cocoa powder

ICING

175 g/6 oz icing sugar, sifted

3 tbsp orange juice

25 g/1 oz plain chocolate, melted

(see pages 9–10)

1 Preheat the oven to 180°C/350°F/Gas Mark 4. Line 2 baking trays with sheets of baking paper.

2 Beat the butter and sugar together until light and fluffy. Beat in the egg and milk until well blended. Sift the flour and cocoa powder together and gradually mix together to form a soft dough. Use your fingers to incorporate the last of the flour and bring the dough together.

3 Roll out the dough on to a lightly floured work surface until 5-mm/¼-inch thick. Using a 5-cm/2-inch fluted round cutter, cut out as many cookies as you can. Re-roll the dough trimmings and cut out more cookies.

Place the cookies on the prepared baking tray, allowing room for expansion during cooking and bake in the preheated oven for 10–12 minutes, or until golden brown.

4 Leave the cookies to cool on the baking tray for a few minutes, then transfer to a wire rack and leave to cool completely.

5 To make the icing, place the icing sugar in a bowl and stir in enough orange juice to form a thin icing that will coat the back of a spoon. Spread the icing over the cookies and leave to set. Drizzle with melted chocolate. Leave to set before serving.

mocha walnut cookies

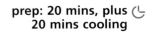

makes about 16 **prep: 20 mins, plus 20 mins cooling** **cook: 10–15 mins**

These cookies have a lovely chewy texture and make a wonderful afternoon treat. They are also ideal for birthday parties.

INGREDIENTS

115 g/4 oz butter, softened, plus extra for greasing

115 g/4 oz light muscovado sugar

85 g/3 oz golden granulated sugar

1 tsp vanilla essence

1 tbsp instant coffee granules, dissolved in 1 tbsp hot water

1 egg

175 g/6 oz plain flour

½ tsp baking powder

¼ tsp bicarbonate of soda

55 g/2 oz milk chocolate chips

55 g/2 oz shelled walnuts, roughly chopped

cook's tip

Muscovado sugar has a tendency to be quite lumpy, so it is a good idea to sift it before use when baking cakes, biscuits and cookies.

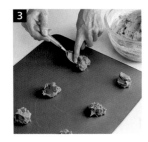

1 Preheat the oven to 180°C/350°F/Gas Mark 4. Grease 2 large baking sheets with a little butter. Place the butter, muscovado sugar and granulated sugar in a large bowl and beat together thoroughly until light and fluffy. Place the vanilla essence, coffee and egg in a separate large bowl and whisk together.

2 Gradually add the coffee mixture to the butter and sugar, beating until fluffy. Sift the flour, baking powder and bicarbonate of soda into the mixture and fold in carefully. Fold in the chocolate chips and walnuts.

3 Drop dessertspoonfuls of the mixture on to the prepared baking sheets,

allowing room for the biscuits to spread. Bake in the hot oven for 10–15 minutes, or until crisp on the outside but still soft inside. Leave to cool on the baking sheets for 2 minutes, then transfer to wire racks to cool completely.

chocolate viennese fingers

⏱ **cook: 15 mins**   🕐 **prep: 20 mins, plus 40 mins cooling/setting**   **makes about 30**

These melt-in-the-mouth biscuits are ideal served with coffee or as an accompaniment to fruit fools and mousses.

cook's tip

Sprinkle some chopped nuts onto the chocolate-coated ends of these biscuits while the chocolate is still soft, if you like.

INGREDIENTS

115 g/4 oz butter, softened, plus extra for greasing

55 g/2 oz golden icing sugar, sifted

125 g/4½ oz plain flour

1 tbsp cocoa powder

100 g/3½ oz plain chocolate, melted and cooled (see pages 9–10)

1 Preheat the oven to 180°C/350°F/Gas Mark 4. Grease 2 baking sheets. Beat the butter and sugar together until light and fluffy. Sift the flour and cocoa powder into the bowl and work the mixture until it is a smooth, piping consistency.

2 Spoon into a large piping bag fitted with a 2.5-cm/1-inch fluted nozzle. Pipe 6-cm/2½-inch lengths of the mixture on to the prepared baking sheets, allowing room for expansion during cooking. Bake in the preheated oven for 15 minutes, or until firm.

3 Leave to cool on the baking sheets for 2 minutes, then transfer to a wire rack to cool completely.

Dip the ends of the biscuits into the melted chocolate and leave to set before serving.

lebkuchen

makes about 60

prep: 20 mins, plus 40 mins cooling/setting

cook: 20–25 mins

These little spicy biscuits are traditionally eaten in Germany on St Nicholas Day, 6 December, but they are great to eat at any time of the year. Serve with freshly brewed coffee.

INGREDIENTS

3 eggs

200 g/7 oz golden caster sugar

55 g/2 oz plain flour

2 tsp cocoa powder

1 tsp ground cinnamon

½ tsp ground cardamom

¼ tsp ground cloves

¼ tsp ground nutmeg

175 g/6 oz ground almonds

55 g/2 oz candied peel, finely chopped

TO DECORATE

115 g/4 oz plain chocolate, melted and cooled (see pages 9–10)

115 g/4 oz white chocolate, melted and cooled (see pages 9–10)

sugar crystals

---

variation

Instead of sprinkling sugar crystals over the finished biscuits, replace with a little sifted icing sugar.

---

cook's tip

After dipping the biscuits in melted chocolate in Step 3, you can leave them to set on greaseproof paper to catch any drips. Store the biscuits in an airtight container for up to 3 days.

1 Preheat the oven to 160°C/325°F/Gas Mark 3. Line several baking sheets with non-stick baking paper. Place the eggs and sugar in a small heatproof bowl and set over a saucepan of gently simmering water. Whisk until thick and foamy. Remove the bowl from the saucepan and continue to whisk for 2 minutes.

2 Sift the flour, cocoa powder, cinnamon, cardamom, cloves and nutmeg over the egg mixture, add the ground almonds and chopped peel and stir. Drop heaped teaspoonfuls of the mixture on to the prepared baking sheets, spreading them gently into smooth mounds and allowing room for expansion during cooking.

3 Bake in the oven for 15–20 minutes, or until light brown and slightly soft to the touch. Leave to cool on the baking sheets for 10 minutes, then transfer to wire racks to cool completely. Dip half the biscuits in the melted plain chocolate and half in the white chocolate. Sprinkle with sugar crystals, leave to set, then serve.

dutch macaroons

cook: 25 mins

prep: 10 mins, plus 40 mins cooling/setting

makes 20

These unusual biscuit treats are delicious served with coffee.
They also make an ideal dessert biscuit to serve with ice cream.

variation

Instead of using plain chocolate, melt 25 g/1 oz white chocolate (see pages 9–10) and drizzle over the top of the cooked macaroons.

cook's tip

Rice paper is edible so you can just break off the excess from around the edge of the biscuits. Remove it completely before dipping in the chocolate, if you prefer.

INGREDIENTS

rice paper

2 egg whites

225 g/8 oz caster sugar

175 g/6 oz ground almonds

225 g/8 oz plain chocolate

1. Preheat the oven to 180°C/350°F/Gas Mark 4. Cover 2 baking trays with rice paper. Whisk the egg whites in a large, clean bowl until stiff, then fold in the sugar and ground almonds.

2. Place the mixture in a large piping bag fitted with a 1-cm/½-inch plain nozzle and pipe fingers, 7.5-cm/3-inches long, allowing room for expansion during cooking.

3. Bake in the hot oven for 15–20 minutes, or until golden. Transfer to a wire rack and leave to cool. Remove the excess rice paper from around the edges.

4. Melt the chocolate (see pages 9–10) and dip the base of each biscuit into the chocolate. Place the macaroons on a sheet of baking paper and leave to set. Drizzle any remaining chocolate over the top of the biscuits (you may have to reheat the chocolate in order to do this). Leave to set before serving.

chocolate & nut crescents

makes about 40

prep: 20 mins, plus 20 mins cooling

cook: 20–25 mins

These crisp little biscuits are a variation on a biscuit that is served in Greece for festivals and special occasions.

INGREDIENTS

225 g/8 oz butter, softened, plus extra for greasing

85 g/3 oz golden caster sugar

1 egg yolk

1 tsp rum

115 g/4 oz shelled walnuts, ground

225 g/8 oz plain flour, plus extra for shaping

55 g/2 oz cornflour

1 tbsp cocoa powder

85 g/3 oz icing sugar, sifted, to coat

variation

For an Italian flavour, replace the rum with 1 tsp of Amaretto liqueur and the walnuts with 115 g/4 oz almonds ground in a food processor.

1 Preheat the oven to 180°C/350°F/Gas Mark 4. Grease several baking sheets. Place the butter and sugar in a bowl and beat together until pale and fluffy. Beat in the egg yolk and rum. Stir in the walnuts. Sift the flour, cornflour and cocoa powder over the mixture and stir, adding a little more flour, if necessary, to make a firm dough.

2 With lightly floured hands, break off walnut-sized pieces of dough and roll into 7.5-cm/3-inch lengths, thick in the centre and tapering into pointed ends. Shape into crescents and place on the prepared baking sheets.

3 Bake in the hot oven for 20–25 minutes, or until firm. Leave to cool on the baking sheets for 2 minutes, then transfer to wire racks to cool completely. Before serving, gently toss the biscuits in a little sifted icing sugar, to coat completely.

nutty chocolate & orange curls

cook: 8–10 mins

prep: 15 mins, plus 15 mins cooling

makes 18

These wafer-thin, crisp, nutty biscuits are ideal for serving with fresh fruit desserts or vanilla ice cream.

cook's tip

Do not be tempted to bake more than one tray of biscuits at a time, otherwise the second batch will become too firm before you have had time to shape them.

INGREDIENTS

55 g/2 oz butter, melted and cooled, plus extra for greasing

2 egg whites

115 g/4 oz golden caster sugar

40 g/1½ oz plain flour

1 tbsp cocoa powder

25 g/1 oz flaked almonds

grated rind of 1 orange

1 Preheat the oven to 180°C/350°F/Gas Mark 4. Grease 2 or 3 baking sheets and a rolling pin with butter. Place the egg whites and sugar in a bowl. Whisk together with a fork until frothy. Sift the flour and cocoa powder into the bowl. Add the almonds and orange rind and mix well. Add the butter and mix together.

2 Drop teaspoonfuls of the mixture on to the prepared baking sheets, allowing plenty of room for expansion during cooking. Using a palette knife, spread each one out slightly. Bake in the preheated oven, one baking sheet at a time, for 8–10 minutes, or until the edges of the biscuits are firm to the touch.

3 Carefully remove the biscuits with a palette knife and place over the prepared rolling pin while still warm. Leave for 1–2 minutes, or until set, then carefully remove and transfer to a wire rack to cool. Store in an airtight container.

hazelnut & chocolate flapjacks

makes 12   **prep: 10 mins, plus ⟳ 30 mins cooling**   **cook: 25–30 mins ⟳**

These chewy, nutty flapjacks are very filling, so they are great for tucking into a lunch box for a sustaining snack on the move.

INGREDIENTS

115 g/4 oz butter, plus extra for greasing

200 g/7 oz porridge oats

55 g/2 oz shelled hazelnuts, lightly toasted and chopped

55 g/2 oz plain flour

85 g/3 oz light muscovado sugar

2 tbsp golden syrup

55 g/2 oz plain chocolate chips

variation

For a special treat, melt 115 g/4 oz plain chocolate (see pages 9–10) and spread over the top of the flapjacks. Leave to set before serving.

1 Preheat the oven to 180°C/350°F/Gas Mark 4. Grease a 23-cm/9-inch shallow square tin with butter. Place the oats, hazelnuts and flour in a large bowl and mix.

2 Place the butter, sugar and syrup in a saucepan and heat gently until the sugar has dissolved. Pour on to the dry ingredients and mix well. Stir in the chocolate chips.

3 Turn the mixture into the prepared tin and bake in the preheated oven for 20–25 minutes, or until golden brown and firm to the touch. Mark into 12 rectangles using a knife and leave to cool in the tin. Cut with a sharp knife, remove from the tin and serve.

chocolate & vanilla pinwheels

cook: 10–15 mins   **prep: 20 mins, plus 1 hr 20 mins chilling/cooling**   **makes about 36**

These two-tone spiral biscuits look impressive and are very simple to make. They look superb arranged in a box and given as a gift.

variation

For a different look, in Step 3, place the vanilla dough on greaseproof paper, then place the chocolate dough on top.

INGREDIENTS

225 g/8 oz butter, softened, plus extra for greasing

115 g/4 oz golden caster sugar

325 g/11½ oz plain flour, plus extra for dusting

1 tbsp cocoa powder

1 tsp vanilla essence

1 Grease 2 or 3 baking sheets with butter. Beat the butter and sugar together until light and fluffy. Transfer half the mixture to a separate bowl and add 150 g/5½ oz of the flour and all of the cocoa powder. Stir the vanilla essence into the other half of the mixture. Sift in the remaining flour. Stir both mixtures to make firm, pliable doughs.

2 Roll out each piece of dough on a floured work surface into a rectangle measuring 20 x 28 cm/ 8 x 11 inches. Place the chocolate dough on a sheet of greaseproof paper and carefully place the vanilla dough on top. Roll up firmly from one long side, using the paper to guide the rolling. Wrap the roll in the paper and leave to chill in the refrigerator for at least 1 hour, or until the dough is firm.

3 Preheat the oven to 180°C/350°F/Gas Mark 4. Unwrap the dough and cut into thin slices. Place the cookies on the prepared baking sheets and bake in the oven for 10–15 minutes, or until golden. Cool on the baking sheets for 2 minutes, then transfer to wire racks to cool completely before serving.

chocolate chip shortbread

serves 8

prep: 10 mins, plus
30 mins cooling

cook: 35–40 mins

Buttery shortbread sprinkled with chocolate chips – nothing could be simpler and more delicious!

INGREDIENTS

115 g/4 oz butter, diced, plus extra
for greasing

115 g/4 oz plain flour

55 g/2 oz cornflour

55 g/2 oz golden caster sugar

40 g/1½ oz plain chocolate chips

variation

To give the shortbread a crunchier texture, use semolina as a substitute for the cornflour. Use milk or white chocolate chips in place of plain.

1 Preheat the oven to 160°C/325°F/Gas Mark 3. Grease a 23-cm/9-inch loose-bottomed fluted flan tin with butter. Sift the flour and cornflour into a large bowl. Stir in the sugar, then add the butter and rub it in until the mixture begins to bind together.

2 Turn into the prepared flan tin and press evenly over the base. Prick the surface with a fork. Sprinkle with the chocolate chips and press lightly into the surface.

3 Bake in the hot oven for 35–40 minutes, or until cooked but not browned.

Mark into 8 portions with a sharp knife. Cool in the tin for 10 minutes, then transfer to a wire rack to cool completely.

cookies & cream sandwiches

🕐 **cook: 20 mins**   🕐 **prep: 25 mins, plus 2 hrs 20 mins cooling/chilling**   **makes 12**

Delicious chocolate shortbread biscuits, with a hint of spice, are sandwiched together with chocolate cream.

cook's tip

Do not sandwich the biscuits together too long before serving, otherwise they will go soft. Store unsandwiched biscuits in an airtight container for up to 3 days.

INGREDIENTS

125 g/4½ oz butter, softened

75 g/2¾ oz golden icing sugar

125 g/4½ oz plain flour

40 g/1½ oz cocoa powder

½ tsp ground cinnamon

FILLING

125 g/4½ oz plain chocolate, broken into pieces

50 ml/2 fl oz double cream

1 Preheat the oven to 160°C/325°F/Gas Mark 3. Line a baking sheet with non-stick baking paper. Place the butter and sugar in a large bowl and beat together until light and fluffy. Sift the flour, cocoa powder and ground cinnamon into the bowl and mix until a smooth dough forms.

2 Place the dough between 2 sheets of non-stick baking paper and roll out to 3 mm/⅛ inch thick. Cut out 6-cm/2½-inch rounds and place on the prepared baking sheet. Bake in the hot oven for 15 minutes, or until firm to the touch. Leave to cool for 2 minutes, then transfer to wire racks to cool completely.

3 To make the filling, place the chocolate and cream in a saucepan and heat gently until the chocolate has melted. Stir until smooth. Leave to cool, then leave to chill in the refrigerator for 2 hours, or until firm. Sandwich the biscuits together in pairs with a spoonful of chocolate cream and serve.

pineapple & cherry florentines

makes about 14   **prep: 15 mins, plus 2 hrs cooling and setting**   **cook: 10–12 mins**

Florentines are a lovely combination of fruit and nuts in a delicate crisp biscuit with a chocolate coating. They are good for serving with vanilla ice cream and also make a welcome gift.

INGREDIENTS

55 g/2 oz butter

40 g/1½ oz demerara sugar

1 tbsp golden syrup

55 g/2 oz plain flour, sifted

25 g/1 oz angelica, roughly chopped

25 g/1 oz glacé cherries, roughly chopped

55 g/2 oz flaked almonds, roughly chopped

55 g/2 oz glacé pineapple, roughly chopped

1 tsp lemon juice

115 g/4 oz plain chocolate, melted and cooled (see pages 9–10)

variation

White chocolate can be used instead of plain. The florentines look attractive if half of them are coated with plain chocolate and half with white.

cook's tip

If you have difficulty removing the florentines from the baking sheet, return to the oven for 2 minutes, then lift off and cool on a wire rack.

1 Preheat the oven to 180°C/350°F/Gas Mark 4. Line several baking sheets with non-stick baking paper. Place the butter, sugar and syrup in a saucepan and heat gently until melted, then stir in the flour, angelica, cherries, almonds, pineapple and lemon juice.

2 Place walnut-sized mounds of the mixture well apart on the baking sheets and flatten with a fork. Bake in the hot oven for 8–10 minutes, or until golden. Use a palette knife to neaten the ragged edges. Leave to cool for 1 minute, then transfer to a wire rack to cool completely.

3 Spread the melted chocolate over the base of each florentine, placing the biscuits, chocolate side up, on a wire rack. Use a fork to mark the chocolate into wavy lines. Leave until set.

ladies' kisses

makes 20   **prep: 30 mins, plus 2 hrs 🕒 30 mins chilling/cooling**   **cook: 30 mins 🕒**

These tiny biscuits sandwiched together with melted chocolate are lovely at teatime or served as petits fours after dinner.

INGREDIENTS

140 g/5 oz unsalted butter

115 g/4 oz caster sugar

1 egg yolk

115 g/4 oz ground almonds

175 g/6 oz plain flour

55 g/2 oz plain chocolate, broken into pieces

2 tbsp icing sugar

2 tbsp cocoa powder

variation

Replace the plain chocolate with the same amount of white chocolate. Omit the icing sugar and use 4 tablespoons cocoa powder for dusting.

cook's tip

Place the dough balls well apart from each other on the baking sheets as they will spread out during cooking. You may need to cook the biscuits in batches.

1 Line 3 baking trays with baking paper, or use 3 non-stick trays. Beat the butter and sugar together in a bowl until pale and fluffy. Beat in the egg yolk, then beat in the almonds and flour. Continue beating until well mixed. Shape the dough into a ball, wrap in clingfilm and leave to chill in the refrigerator for 1½–2 hours.

2 Preheat the oven to 160°C/325°F/Gas Mark 3. Unwrap the dough, break off walnut-sized pieces and roll them into balls between the palms of your hands. Place the dough balls on the prepared baking trays, allowing room for expansion during cooking. Bake in the preheated oven for 20–25 minutes, or until golden brown. Carefully transfer the biscuits, still on the baking paper, if using, to wire racks to cool.

3 Place the plain chocolate in a small heatproof bowl and set over a saucepan of barely simmering water, stirring constantly until melted. Remove the bowl from the heat.

4 Remove the biscuits from the baking paper, if using, and spread the melted chocolate over the bases. Sandwich them together in pairs and return to the wire racks to cool. Dust with a mixture of icing sugar and cocoa powder and serve.

tiffin

cook: 5 mins   **prep: 10 mins, plus 9 hrs 30 mins soaking/chilling**   **makes 12 pieces**

Tiffin is a wonderful uncooked biscuit cake containing plain chocolate, dried fruit and nuts. You can cut it into smaller pieces to serve with after-dinner coffee.

variation

If this is to be served to children, use orange juice instead of brandy for soaking the raisins.

cook's tip

For a decorative effect, use a fork to lightly mark wavy lines over the chocolate topping before leaving it to set in the refrigerator overnight.

INGREDIENTS

55 g/2 oz butter, plus extra for greasing
55 g/2 oz raisins
2 tbsp brandy
115 g/4 oz plain chocolate, broken into pieces
115 g/4 oz milk chocolate, broken into pieces
2 tbsp golden syrup
175 g/6 oz digestive biscuits, roughly broken

55 g/2 oz flaked almonds, lightly toasted
25 g/1 oz glacé cherries, chopped

TOPPING
100 g/3½ oz plain chocolate, broken into pieces
20 g/¾ oz butter

1 Grease and line the base of an 18-cm/ 7-inch shallow square tin. Place the raisins and brandy in a bowl and leave to soak for 30 minutes. Put the chocolate, butter and syrup in a saucepan and heat gently until melted.

2 Stir in the digestive biscuits, almonds, cherries, raisins and brandy.

Turn into the prepared tin and leave to cool. Cover and leave to chill in the refrigerator for 1 hour.

3 To make the topping, place the chocolate and butter in a small heatproof bowl and set over a saucepan of gently simmering water until melted. Stir and pour over the biscuit base. Leave to

chill in the refrigerator for 8 hours, or overnight. Cut into bars or squares to serve.

no-bake chocolate squares

makes 16 **prep: 10 mins, plus 2 hrs** ↻ **20 mins chilling/setting** **cook: 5 mins** ⏲

Children will enjoy making these as an introduction to chocolate cooking, and they keep well in the refrigerator.

INGREDIENTS

275 g/9½ oz plain chocolate

175 g/6 oz butter

4 tbsp golden syrup

2 tbsp dark rum (optional)

175 g/6 oz plain biscuits, such as Rich Tea

25 g/1 oz toasted rice cereal

50 g/1¾ oz chopped walnuts or pecan nuts

100 g/3½ oz glacé cherries, roughly chopped

25 g/1 oz white chocolate, to decorate

variation

Brandy or an orange-flavoured liqueur can be used instead of the rum, if you prefer. Cherry brandy also works well.

1 Line an 18-cm/7-inch square cake tin with baking paper. Place the plain chocolate in a large bowl with the butter, syrup and rum, if using, and set over a saucepan of gently simmering water until melted, stirring constantly, until blended.

2 Break the biscuits into small pieces and stir

into the chocolate mixture with the rice cereal, nuts and cherries.

3 Pour the mixture into the tin and smooth the top, pressing down well with the back of a spoon. Leave to chill in the refrigerator for 2 hours.

4 To decorate, melt the white chocolate (see pages 9–10) and drizzle it over the top of the cake in a random pattern. Leave to set. To serve, carefully turn out of the tin and remove the baking paper. Cut into 16 squares and serve.

caramel chocolate shortbread

makes 24   **prep: 10 mins, plus** ⏲ **1 hr chilling/setting**   **cook: 30 mins** ⏱

This is a truly luxurious shortbread, combined with a sumptuous layer of caramel topped with crisp chocolate.

INGREDIENTS

115 g/4 oz butter, plus extra for greasing

175 g/6 oz plain flour

55 g/2 oz golden caster sugar

FILLING AND TOPPING

175 g/6 oz butter

115 g/4 oz golden caster sugar

3 tbsp golden syrup

400 g/14 oz canned condensed milk

200 g/7 oz plain chocolate, broken into pieces

variation

If you cannot find golden caster sugar, then use ordinary caster sugar instead. Replace the plain chocolate topping with white or milk chocolate.

cook's tip

Take great care when cooking the caramel filling as it can very easily catch and burn on the base of the saucepan. Stir the mixture constantly until it has thickened.

1 Preheat the oven to180°C/350°F/Gas Mark 4. Grease and line the base of a 23-cm/9-inch shallow square cake tin. Place the butter, flour and sugar in a food processor and process until it begins to bind together. Press the mixture into the tin and smooth the top. Bake in the preheated oven, for 20–25 minutes, or until golden.

2 Meanwhile, make the filling. Place the butter, sugar, syrup and condensed milk in a saucepan and heat gently until the sugar has melted. Bring to the boil and simmer for 6–8 minutes, stirring constantly, until the mixture becomes very thick. Pour over the shortbread base and leave to chill in the refrigerator until firm.

3 To make the topping, melt the chocolate (see pages 9–10) and leave to cool, then spread over the caramel. Chill in the refrigerator until set. Cut the shortbread into 12 pieces with a sharp knife and serve.

chocolate crispy bites

🕘 **cook: 10 mins**   🕘 **prep: 45 mins, plus 2 hrs chilling**   **makes 16**

A favourite with children, this version of crispy bites has been given a new twist, which is sure to be very popular.

variation

For a change, place a spoonful of the white chocolate mixture in paper cake cases and top with a spoonful of the plain chocolate. Chill until hardened.

cook's tip

These crispy bites can be made up to 4 days ahead. Keep them covered in the refrigerator until ready to use, then cut into small squares and serve.

INGREDIENTS

WHITE LAYER	DARK LAYER
4 tbsp butter, plus extra for greasing	4 tbsp butter
1 tbsp golden syrup	2 tbsp golden syrup
150 g/5½ oz white chocolate, broken into small pieces	125 g/4½ oz plain chocolate, broken into small pieces
50 g/1¾ oz toasted rice cereal	75 g/2¾ oz toasted rice cereal

1 Grease a 20-cm/8-inch square cake tin and line with baking paper. To make the white chocolate layer, place the butter, syrup and chocolate in a heatproof bowl and set over a saucepan of gently simmering water until melted. Remove from the heat and stir in the rice cereal until well blended. Press into the tin and smooth the surface.

2 To make the dark chocolate layer, place the butter, syrup and plain chocolate in a heatproof bowl and set over a saucepan of gently simmering water until melted.

3 Remove the saucepan from the heat and stir in the rice cereal until well blended. Pour the dark chocolate layer over the white chocolate layer, and leave to chill in the refrigerator for 2 hours, or until hardened. Turn out of the cake tin and cut into small squares, using a sharp knife.

panforte di siena

serves 12–16   **prep: 10 mins, plus 20 mins cooling**   **cook: 35–40 mins**

Chewy, sticky panforte is the traditional Christmas cake of Siena. Chocolate was first added to the recipe when cocoa arrived from the New World, and became the fashionable ingredient.

INGREDIENTS

butter, for greasing
55 g/2 oz glacé cherries, quartered
115 g/4 oz mixed candied orange and lemon peel, finely chopped
25 g/1 oz crystallized ginger, roughly chopped
115 g/4 oz flaked almonds
115 g/4 oz hazelnuts, toasted and roughly ground
55 g/2 oz plain flour

25 g/1 oz cocoa powder
1 tsp ground cinnamon
¼ tsp ground cloves
¼ tsp ground nutmeg
¼ tsp ground coriander
115 g/4 oz clear honey
115 g/4 oz golden caster sugar
1 tsp orange flower water
icing sugar, for dusting

variation

You can replace the glacé cherries with dried cranberries and the crystallized ginger with the same amount of crystallized pineapple.

cook's tip

Panforte will keep in an airtight container for up to 2 months. Do not store it in a plastic container, otherwise the panforte may taste musty. Sift with extra icing sugar before serving.

1 Preheat the oven to 160°C/325°F/Gas Mark 3. Thoroughly grease the base of a 20-cm/8-inch loose-bottomed cake or flan tin. Line the base with non-stick baking paper. Place the cherries, candied peel, ginger, almonds and hazelnuts in a bowl. Sift in the flour, cocoa powder, cinnamon, cloves, nutmeg and coriander and mix. Reserve.

2 Place the honey, sugar and orange flower water in a saucepan and heat gently until the sugar has dissolved. Bring the mixture to the boil and boil steadily until a temperature of 116°C/241°F has been reached on a sugar thermometer, or a small amount of the mixture forms a soft ball when dropped into cold water.

3 Quickly remove the saucepan from the heat and stir in the dry ingredients. Mix thoroughly and turn into the prepared tin. Spread evenly and bake in the oven for 30 minutes. Leave to cool in the tin. Turn out and carefully peel away the lining paper. Dust icing sugar lightly over the top and cut into wedges to serve.

sweets & drinks

It is surprising just how easy sweets are to make at home, and how delicious! They will always bring a touch of luxury and sophistication to a dinner party, and the fact that they can be made in advance is an added bonus when entertaining. Try the decorative Chocolate Orange Collettes (see page 230) or the irresistible Chocolate-Dipped Fruit (see page 240), which makes an ideal light alternative to a traditional festive dessert. Home-made chocolates, attractively packaged, also make much-appreciated Christmas and birthday gifts. Irish Cream Truffles (see page 234) are extravagantly rich, while Pecan Mocha Fudge (see page 236) will delight the fudge-lover in your family.

Chocolate lends itself particularly well to warming drinks, and mixes deliciously with a whole variety of liqueurs and spirits. Mexicana (see page 250) is an ambrosial combination of coffee, chocolate and whipped cream, while Café Mocha (see page 253) is set off seductively with coffee-flavoured ice cream. Children will love the Quick Chocolate Milk Shake (see page 248) – even the reluctant milk-drinkers!

chocolate orange collettes

🔥 **cook: 5–10 mins**   ⏲ **prep: 40 mins, plus 2 hrs chilling**   **makes 20**

Delicate chocolate cases filled with a soft, deliciously rich truffle mixture look as good as they taste.

variation
Make some or all of the chocolate cases with white chocolate, or use white chocolate in some or all of the filling, if you like.

cook's tip
To get fine strips of orange rind, either use a zester or cut into thin strips with a vegetable peeler and shred into fine strips.

INGREDIENTS

280 g/10 oz plain chocolate,
broken into pieces
½ tsp sunflower oil
150 ml/5 fl oz double cream
finely grated rind of ½ orange
1 tbsp Cointreau

TO DECORATE
chopped nuts
fine strips of orange rind

1 Melt 150 g/5½ oz of the chocolate with the oil (see pages 9–10) and stir until mixed. Spread evenly over the inside of 20 double petit four cases, taking care to keep a good thickness around the edge. Chill for 1 hour, or until set, then apply a second coat of chocolate, re-melting if necessary. Chill for 1 hour, or until completely set.

2 Place the cream and grated orange rind in a saucepan and heat until almost boiling. Remove from the heat, add the remaining chocolate pieces and stir until smooth. Return to the heat and stir until the mixture begins to bubble. Remove from the heat and stir in the Cointreau. Leave to cool. Peel the paper cases off the chocolate cups.

3 Beat the chocolate cream until thick, then spoon into a large piping bag fitted with a fluted nozzle. Pipe the chocolate cream into the chocolate cases. Decorate some of the chocolate collettes with chopped nuts and some with a few strips of orange rind. Cover and keep in the fridge. Use within 2–3 days.

rum & chocolate cups

serves 12   prep: 25 mins, plus 2 hrs ⟲ chilling/cooling   cook: 10–15 mins ⟳

Use firm foil confectionery cases, rather than paper ones, to make the chocolate cups, because they offer extra support.

INGREDIENTS

55 g/2 oz plain chocolate, broken into pieces

12 toasted hazelnuts

FILLING

115 g/4 oz plain chocolate, broken into pieces

1 tbsp dark rum

4 tbsp mascarpone cheese

---

variation

For a change, replace the plain chocolate in the filling for the same amount of white chocolate.

---

cook's tip

When melting the chocolate in Step 1, stir the chocolate thoroughly until it is melted and smooth, but not too runny, otherwise it will be difficult to coat the cases.

1 To make the chocolate cups, place the plain chocolate in the top of a double boiler or in a heatproof bowl set over a saucepan of barely simmering water. Stir over a low heat until the chocolate is just melted but not too runny, then remove from the heat. Spoon ½ teaspoon of melted chocolate into a foil confectionery case and brush it over the base and up the sides. Coat 11 more foil cases in the same way and leave for 30 minutes to set. Chill in the refrigerator for 15 minutes. If necessary, reheat the chocolate in the double boiler or heatproof bowl to melt it again, then coat the foil cases with a second, slightly thinner coating. Chill in the refrigerator for a further 30 minutes.

2 Meanwhile, make the filling. Place the chocolate in the top of a double boiler or in a small heatproof bowl set over a saucepan of barely simmering water. Stir over a low heat until melted and smooth, then remove from the heat. Leave to cool slightly, then stir in the rum and beat in the mascarpone cheese until fully incorporated and smooth. Leave to cool completely, stirring occasionally.

3 Spoon the filling into a piping bag fitted with a 1-cm/½-inch star nozzle. Carefully peel away the confectionery cases from the chocolate cups. Pipe the filling into the cups and top each one with a toasted hazelnut.

irish cream truffles

makes about 24

prep: 35 mins, plus 10–12 hrs chilling

cook: 5–10 mins

Truffles are simple to make and will impress your guests at the end of a dinner party. They are also the ideal gift for chocoholics.

INGREDIENTS

150 ml/5 fl oz double cream

225 g/8 oz plain chocolate, broken into pieces

25 g/1 oz butter

3 tbsp Irish cream liqueur

115 g/4 oz white chocolate, broken into pieces

115 g/4 oz plain chocolate, broken into pieces

variation

Brandy, rum or Grand Marnier can be used instead of Irish cream liqueur. After coating the truffles in chocolate, roll them in chopped nuts.

cook's tip

If the truffle mixture is too firm to roll into small balls when it comes out of the refrigerator, leave it to soften at room temperature for a few minutes.

1 Heat the cream in a saucepan over a low heat but do not let it boil. Remove from the heat and stir in the chocolate and butter. Leave for 2 minutes, then stir until smooth. Stir in the liqueur. Pour the mixture into a bowl and leave to cool. Cover and chill in the refrigerator for 8 hours, or overnight, until firm.

2 Line a baking sheet with non-stick baking paper. Take teaspoonfuls of the chilled chocolate mixture and roll into small balls. Place the balls on the prepared baking sheet and leave to chill in the refrigerator for 2–4 hours, or until firm. Melt the white chocolate pieces (see pages 9–10) and leave to cool slightly.

3 Coat half the truffles by spearing on thin skewers or cocktail sticks and dipping into the white chocolate. Transfer to a sheet of non-stick baking paper to set. Melt the plain chocolate and leave to cool slightly, then use to coat the remaining truffles in the same way. Store the truffles in the refrigerator in an airtight container, separated by layers of greaseproof paper, for up to 1 week.

white chocolate & pistachio truffles

cook: 5 mins

prep: 30 mins, plus 10 hrs chilling

makes 26–30

These wickedly rich truffles add a touch of decadence to the end of a light meal. They look attractive arranged in a glass serving dish.

variation

Use ready-flavoured chocolate, such as coffee, mint or orange, combined with chopped hazelnuts, walnuts or almonds.

cook's tip

The truffles look best if they are quite rough, rather than being rolled into smooth balls. Roll the truffles lightly in the icing sugar, otherwise they will taste very sweet.

INGREDIENTS

100 g/3½ oz white chocolate, broken into pieces

15 g/½ oz butter

75 ml/2½ fl oz double cream

25 g/1 oz shelled unsalted pistachio nuts, finely chopped

icing sugar, to coat

1 Place the chocolate, butter and cream in a heatproof bowl and set over a saucepan of gently simmering water until melted, without stirring. Remove the bowl from the heat and stir gently, then stir in the nuts. Leave to cool,

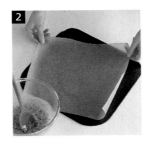

then cover with clingfilm and leave to chill in the refrigerator for 8 hours, or overnight.

2 Line a baking sheet with non-stick baking paper. Take teaspoonfuls of the mixture and roll into balls.

Place the truffles on the prepared baking sheet and chill in the refrigerator for 2 hours, or until firm.

3 Just before serving, roll the truffles in icing sugar to coat.

pecan mocha fudge

cook: 15–20 mins   **prep: 15 mins, plus 2 hrs setting**   **makes 80 pieces**

This recipe makes plenty of delicious fudge for eating yourself, for sharing and for giving away as presents!

variation

Chopped unsalted pistachio nuts, Brazil nuts, almonds or walnuts can be used instead of the pecan nuts.

cook's tip

To test the temperature of the fudge accurately, it is best to use a sugar thermometer. These are available from specialist kitchen shops.

INGREDIENTS

250 g/9 oz butter, plus extra
for greasing

300 ml/10 fl oz milk

1 kg/2 lb 4 oz golden granulated sugar

2 tbsp instant coffee granules

2 tbsp cocoa powder

2 tbsp golden syrup

400 g/14 oz canned condensed milk

115 g/4 oz shelled pecan nuts, chopped

1 Grease a 30 x 23-cm/ 12 x 9-inch Swiss roll tin. Place the milk, sugar and butter in a large saucepan. Stir over a gentle heat until the sugar has dissolved. Stir in the coffee granules, cocoa powder, syrup and condensed milk.

2 Bring to the boil and boil steadily, whisking constantly, for 10 minutes, or until a temperature of 116°C/ 241°F has been reached on a sugar thermometer, or a small amount of the mixture forms a soft ball when dropped into cold water.

3 Leave to cool for 5 minutes, then beat vigorously with a wooden spoon until the mixture begins to thicken. Stir in the nuts.

Continue beating until the mixture takes on a fudge-like consistency. Quickly pour into the prepared tin and leave in a cool place to set. Cut the fudge into squares to serve.

easy chocolate fudge

makes 25 pieces   **prep: 10 mins, plus** ⏲ **1 hr chilling**   **cook: 5–10 mins** ⏲

This is the easiest fudge to make – for a really rich flavour, use a good-quality plain chocolate with a high cocoa content, ideally at least 70 per cent.

INGREDIENTS

75 g/2¾ oz unsalted butter, cut into
even-sized pieces, plus extra
for greasing
500 g/1 lb 2 oz plain chocolate
400 g/14 oz canned condensed milk
½ tsp vanilla essence

variation

Replace the vanilla essence with
1 teaspoon rum. Add the rum with the
butter and condensed milk in Step 1.

cook's tip

If there is any left, you can store the
fudge in an airtight container in a cool,
dry place for up to 1 month.
Do not freeze.

1 Lightly grease a
20-cm/8-inch square
cake tin with butter. Break the
chocolate into small pieces and
place in a large, heavy-based
saucepan with the butter and
condensed milk.

2 Heat gently, stirring
constantly, until the
chocolate and butter melt and
the mixture is smooth. Do not
allow to boil. Remove from the
heat. Beat in the vanilla
essence, then beat the mixture
for a few minutes until
thickened. Pour it into the tin
and smooth the top.

3 Leave the mixture to
chill in the refrigerator
for 1 hour, or until firm. Tip
the fudge out on to a
chopping board and cut into
squares to serve.

chocolate-dipped fruit

serves 4 · prep: 15 mins, plus 🕐 30 mins chilling · cook: 5 mins 🕐

Fresh fruit dipped in chocolate looks attractive and is less rich than ordinary chocolates, making it an ideal treat to serve with coffee at the end of a heavy meal.

INGREDIENTS

12 large cherries, with stalks attached

12 Cape gooseberries

200 g/7 oz plain chocolate, broken into pieces

1 tbsp sunflower oil

variation
Small strawberries would make a good alternative or addition to the cherries and Cape gooseberries.

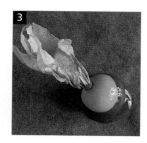

1 Line a baking sheet with non-stick baking paper. Wash and dry the cherries. Peel back the papery outer case from the Cape gooseberries and twist at the top to make a 'handle'.

2 Place the chocolate and oil in a small heatproof bowl and set over a saucepan of gently simmering water until the chocolate has melted. Remove from the heat, stir to mix, then leave to cool until tepid. Dip the fruit in the chocolate and let any excess drain back into the saucepan. The fruit does not need to be completely coated.

3 Set the fruit on the prepared baking sheet. If the chocolate forms a 'foot' on the paper, it is too warm, so leave it to cool slightly. If the chocolate in the bowl begins to set, warm it gently over the saucepan of simmering water. Chill the dipped fruit in the refrigerator for 30 minutes, or until the chocolate is set, then peel away from the paper. Serve on their own, or use to decorate another dessert.

chocolate marzipans

cook: 10 mins

prep: 40 mins, plus 2 hrs chilling

makes 30

These delightful little marzipans make the perfect gift, if you can resist eating them all yourself! Alternatively, arrange on a serving plate and serve with coffee as an after-dinner treat.

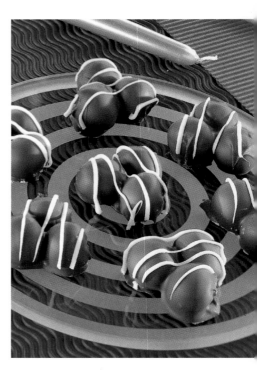

variation

Coat the marzipan balls in white or milk chocolate and drizzle with plain chocolate, if you prefer.

INGREDIENTS

450 g/1 lb marzipan

25 g/1 oz glacé cherries, very finely chopped

icing sugar, for dusting

25 g/1 oz stem ginger, very finely chopped

50 g/1¾ oz ready-to-eat dried apricots, very finely chopped

350 g/12 oz plain chocolate, broken into pieces

25 g/1 oz white chocolate

1 Line a baking tray with non-stick baking paper. Divide the marzipan into 3 balls and knead each ball to soften it.

2 Work the glacé cherries into 1 portion of the marzipan by kneading on a work surface lightly dusted with icing sugar. Do the same with the stem ginger and another portion of marzipan, then the apricots and the third portion of marzipan. Form each flavoured portion of marzipan into small balls, keeping the flavours separate.

3 Place the plain chocolate in a heatproof bowl and set over a saucepan of hot water. Stir until the chocolate has melted.

4 Dip one of each flavoured ball of marzipan into the melted chocolate by spiking each one with a cocktail stick, allowing the excess chocolate to drip back into the bowl.

4 Place the balls in clusters of the 3 flavours on the baking tray. Repeat with the remaining balls. Leave to chill in the refrigerator for 1 hour, or until set. Place the white chocolate in a small heatproof bowl and set over a saucepan of simmering water. Stir until the chocolate has melted. Drizzle a little over the tops of each cluster of marzipan balls. Chill in the refrigerator for 1 hour, or until hardened, then remove from the baking paper, arrange on a plate and serve.

apricot & almond clusters

cook: 5 mins **prep: 10 mins, plus 2–4 hrs setting** **makes 24–28**

These delicious little morsels are extremely quick and easy to make.
They are perfect for an after dinner treat with coffee.

variation

Dates would also work well in this recipe. Replace the apricots with the same amount of chopped, ready-to-eat dates.

cook's tip

These are easy sweets for children to make, as long as they have some help with melting the chocolate.

INGREDIENTS

115 g/4 oz plain chocolate,
broken into pieces
2 tbsp clear honey
115 g/4 oz no-soak dried
apricots, chopped
55 g/2 oz blanched almonds, chopped

1 Place the chocolate and honey in a heatproof bowl and set over a saucepan of gently simmering water until the chocolate has melted.

2 Stir the apricots and almonds into the melted chocolate mixture.

3 Drop teaspoonfuls of the mixture into petit four cases. Leave to set for 2–4 hours, or until firm. Serve.

torrone molle

makes 24 pieces   **prep: 30 mins, plus 8 hrs chilling**   **cook: 15 mins**

This is a delicious Italian speciality, which is a rich mixture of good-quality plain chocolate, ground nuts and plain biscuits.

INGREDIENTS

oil, for brushing

175 g/6 oz butter, softened

175 g/6 oz plain chocolate, melted (see pages 9–10)

55 g/2 oz shelled walnuts, roughly ground

55 g/2 oz blanched almonds, roughly ground

55 g/2 oz shelled hazelnuts, roughly ground

115 g/4 oz golden caster sugar

3 tbsp water

1 tbsp brandy

175 g/6 oz plain biscuits, such as Petit Beurre

variation

If you like, substitute rum for the brandy and ground pecan nuts for the ground hazelnuts.

cook's tip

If you are grinding the nuts yourself in a food processor, take care not to overprocess them or they will become too oily and may spoil the finished dish.

1 Brush a 28 x 20-cm/ 11 x 8-inch Swiss roll tin with oil. Place the softened butter in a bowl, add the melted chocolate and beat together until smooth. Stir in the walnuts, almonds and hazelnuts. Place the sugar and water in a heavy-based saucepan and heat until the sugar has dissolved.

2 Boil the mixture steadily until a temperature of 116°C/241°F has been reached on a sugar thermometer, or a small amount of the mixture forms a soft ball when dropped into cold water. Leave to cool for a few minutes, then beat vigorously. Pour into the chocolate mixture, stirring constantly, until smooth.

3 Stir in the brandy. Break the biscuits into small almond-sized pieces and stir gently into the mixture. Turn into the prepared tin and press to flatten. Cover and chill in the refrigerator for 8 hours, or overnight. Remove from the refrigerator just before serving and cut into diamond shapes.

mini chocolate cones

makes 10

prep: 40 mins, plus
3–4 hrs chilling

cook: 5 mins

These unusual cone-shaped mint-cream chocolates make a change from the more usual cup shape, and are perfect as an after-dinner chocolate with coffee or liqueurs.

INGREDIENTS

75 g/2¾ oz plain chocolate

100 ml/3½ fl oz double cream

1 tbsp icing sugar

1 tbsp crème de menthe

chocolate-covered coffee beans,
to decorate (optional)

cook's tip

The chocolate cones can be made in advance and kept in the refrigerator for up to 1 week. Do not fill them more than 2 hours before you are going to serve them.

1 Cut 10 x 7.5-cm/3-inch circles of baking paper. Shape each circle into a cone shape and secure with a piece of sticky tape.

2 Break the chocolate into pieces, place in a heatproof bowl and set over a saucepan of hot water. Stir until the chocolate has melted.

Using a small pastry brush or clean artists' brush, brush the inside of each cone with the melted chocolate.

3 Brush a second layer of chocolate on the inside of the cones and leave to chill in the refrigerator for 2 hours, or until set. Carefully peel away the paper.

4 Place the cream, icing sugar and crème de menthe in a large bowl and whip until just holding its shape. Place in a piping bag fitted with a star nozzle and pipe the mixture into the chocolate cones.

5 Decorate the cones with chocolate-covered coffee beans, if using, and leave to chill in the refrigerator for 1–2 hours, until required.

brazil nut brittle

⏱ **cook: 10 mins**   ⏱ **prep: 20 mins, plus 30 mins setting**   **makes 20**

Chunks of fudge, white chocolate and Brazil nuts are embedded in plain chocolate. For the best results, choose the highest-quality plain chocolate that you can find.

cook's tip

Place the brittle on a serving plate or in an airtight container and keep, covered, in a cool place. Alternatively, store in the refrigerator for up to 3 days.

INGREDIENTS

oil, for oiling

350 g/12 oz plain chocolate, broken into pieces

85 g/3 oz shelled Brazil nuts, chopped

175 g/6 oz white chocolate, roughly chopped

175 g/6 oz fudge, roughly chopped

1 Oil and line the base of a 20-cm/8-inch square cake tin with non-stick baking paper. Melt half the plain chocolate (see pages 9–10) and spread in the prepared tin.

2 Sprinkle with the Brazil nuts, white chocolate and fudge. Melt the remaining plain chocolate (see pages 9–10) and pour over the top.

3 Leave to set, then break into jagged pieces using the tip of a strong knife.

quick chocolate milk shake

serves 2　　　　　**prep: 5 mins** ⏻　　　　　**cook: 0 mins** ⏱

This is a great way to encourage children to drink milk, although adults will also enjoy this drink.

INGREDIENTS

6 rounded tbsp vanilla ice cream

4 tbsp drinking chocolate

300 ml/10 fl oz milk

1 chocolate flake bar, roughly crushed

ground cinnamon, for dusting

variation
For a more chocolatey milk shake, use chocolate ice cream instead of vanilla, and decorate the top with a light dusting of cocoa powder.

1 Place the vanilla ice cream, drinking chocolate and milk in a blender or food processor.

2 Process the mixture for 30 seconds, then pour into 2 tall serving glasses.

3 Sprinkle with the flake, add a light dusting of cinnamon and serve with straws, if you like.

real hot chocolate

cook: 5 mins   **prep: 5 mins**   **serves 1–2**

You will never go back to commercial drinking chocolate once you have tasted this! Choose the best-quality chocolate you can buy.

variation
Chocolate powder for dusting on cappuccino is available in most large supermarkets alongside the coffee. Alternatively, use drinking chocolate or cocoa powder.

INGREDIENTS

40 g/1½ oz plain chocolate, broken into pieces

300 ml/10 fl oz milk

2 tbsp whipped cream, to decorate

chocolate powder, for dusting

1 Place the chocolate in a large, heatproof jug. Place the milk in a heavy-based saucepan and bring to the boil. Pour about one-quarter of the milk on to the chocolate and leave until the chocolate has softened.

2 Whisk the milk and chocolate mixture until smooth. Return the remaining milk to the heat and return to the boil, then pour on to the chocolate, whisking constantly.

3 Pour into warmed mugs or cups and top with whipped cream dusted with chocolate powder. Serve immediately.

mexicana

serves 2　　　　　　　**prep: 5 mins** ⏲　　　　　　　**cook: 0 mins** ⏱

Chocolate, coffee and rum make this a drink to really lift the spirits. It looks particularly attractive served in tall, heatproof glasses.

INGREDIENTS

25 g/1 oz plain chocolate

300 ml/10 fl oz hot black coffee

25 g/1 oz golden caster sugar

1 tbsp rum

TO DECORATE

2 tbsp whipped cream

ground coffee

---

variation

If your time is limited, you can use ready-to-serve whipped cream, which is sold in cans. Just shake the can well, squirt on top of the drink and serve.

1 Place the chocolate, coffee and sugar in a blender or food processor.

2 Process until well blended, then add the rum, stir, and pour into 2 tall, heatproof glasses.

3 Top with whipped cream and sprinkle with a little ground coffee. Serve immediately.

chocolate eggnog

⏱ **cook: 5 mins**   ⏲ **prep: 15 mins**   **serves 4**

The perfect pick-me-up on a cold winter's night, this delicious drink will get the taste buds tingling.

cook's tip
If you don't have any rum, then you can use brandy instead. Try to use a good-quality plain chocolate for grating over the drink.

INGREDIENTS

8 egg yolks

200 g/7 oz sugar

1 litre/1¾ pints milk

225 g/8 oz plain chocolate, grated

150 ml/5 fl oz dark rum

1 Place the egg yolks and sugar in a large bowl and, using an electric mixer, mix until thickened.

2 Pour the milk into a large, heavy-based saucepan, add the grated plain chocolate and bring to the boil.

3 Remove the saucepan from the heat and gradually mix into the egg yolk mixture. Stir in the rum, pour into heatproof glasses and serve immediately.

hot brandy chocolate

Brandy and chocolate have a natural affinity with one another, as this richly flavoured drink amply demonstrates.

INGREDIENTS

1 litre/1¾ pints milk

115 g/4 oz plain chocolate, broken into pieces

2 tbsp sugar

5 tbsp brandy

TO DECORATE

6 tbsp whipped cream

4 tsp cocoa powder

cook's tip

When melting chocolate and milk, always use a heavy-based saucepan and stir constantly to prevent the chocolate and milk burning on the base of the saucepan.

1 Pour the milk into a large, heavy-based saucepan and bring to the boil over a low heat. As soon as it reaches boiling point, remove the saucepan from the heat.

2 Place the chocolate in a small saucepan and add 2 tablespoons of the milk. Stir over a low heat until the chocolate has melted, then stir the chocolate mixture into the remaining milk. Add the sugar.

3 Stir in the brandy and pour into 4 tall, heatproof glasses. Top each with a swirl of whipped cream and sprinkle with a little sifted cocoa powder. Serve immediately.

café mocha

cook: 5 mins　　　**prep: 5 mins**　　　**serves 2**

This is sheer indulgence for coffee- and chocolate-lovers alike.
Choose the best-quality ice cream or even make your own.

variation

For a change, replace the coffee ice cream with chocolate or vanilla ice cream, if you like.

INGREDIENTS

55 g/2 oz plain chocolate,
broken into pieces
2 tbsp water
2 tbsp golden caster sugar
225 ml/8 fl oz milk
125 ml/4 fl oz freshly made strong
black coffee
2 scoops of coffee ice cream
2 tbsp whipped cream, to decorate

1 Place the chocolate, water and sugar in a large, heavy-based saucepan and heat gently until melted. Stir until smooth. Reserve a little sauce for decoration.

2 Stir the milk into the chocolate sauce. Divide the coffee between 2 tall, warmed, heatproof glasses and pour the chocolate mixture over.

3 Add the ice cream and drizzle the reserved chocolate sauce over. Top each glass with a tablespoonful of cream and serve immediately.

index